# THE

# *Handwriting*

# IS ON

# THE

# WALL

## DR. GEORGE B. JACKSON

foreword by Dr. Dee Stokes

*To Paulette,*
*Grace and Peace Multiplied*
*Jackso*
*7•24•22*

Scriptures taken from the Holy Bible, New King James Version © 1982 unless otherwise noted.

Editor & Book Cover Design – Pamela S. Jackson

*Pureheart Publishing Inc.*
*Thomasville, NC 27360*


ISBN: 9781070575148

# MEMOIRS OF A GOSPEL PREACHER

VOLUME 3

*"In the same hour the fingers of a man's hand appeared and wrote opposite the lampstand on the plaster of the wall of the king's palace; and the king saw the part of the hand that wrote."*

*~ Daniel 5:5 NKJV*

# Dedication

To my grandchildren Amani Joy, Sterling Xavier, Njeri Anaya,
Salina Auset, Arrianna Nicole and Antoine Kedar.
I'm expecting great things from great people like you.
Love Always,
Pop Pop

# Acknowledgments

Special thanks to my wife, Dr. Pamela S. Jackson, and Pureheart Publishing for pushing me to meet deadlines and complete the assignment. Thank you to Citadel of Faith Christian Fellowship for tolerating me for almost 20 years. Thank you Citadel Ministries International for walking with me since 2013. God bless United Cornerstone University, Board of Trustees, Administration, Faculty, Beloved Alumni and students for having the unmitigated gall; "To Learn, To Love, To Be."

# Foreword

Everyone loves a good story and one they can understand and relate to their own lives. Dr. George B. Jackson is one of the best teachers and storytellers I have ever heard. The expository preacher sets the story in motion and makes it come alive to give the audience a real taste of what the Biblical text is serving. Bishop Jackson exhibits theological precision when exegeting texts of Scripture and he makes the narrative real as if we were in the Biblical world hearing it for the first time.

In "The Handwriting is on the Wall," Bishop Jackson gives the reader several sections in order to understand the Biblical text, and produce a well-prepared sermon for all ears. Dr. Jackson has broken down each pericope and given us a playbook to follow. Each message contains an introduction, exposition, exegesis, questions to answer, and a conclusion. There are four total parts to the book that build up to a stunning finale. Part One focuses on the challenges of today that face the Lord's Church and His people and teaches on exposition. Part Two challenges us to use our authority in Christ and be bold and passionate people and focuses on the technique of labeling. Part Three is a sobering account of Jesus' walk to the cross and urges us to preach "Christ and Him crucified" and directs us to writing a powerful introduction. The Fourth and final part has the 1st Century Church in view and highlights many of the same issues the 21st Century Church deals with today and focuses on a conclusion or finale that will wrap up the sermon.

"The Handwriting is on the Wall" is a great resource for preachers of all ages and skill level. This book will be valuable for preachers to have in their library and to refer to often. Thank you Dr. Jackson for writing it.

Dr. Dee Stokes
Preacher, Author, & President/CEO
Dee Stokes Ministries, Inc.

# Table of Contents

# CAN YOU HEAR THE RUMBLE?

Part One
Prophetic Rumblings

## Prophetic Rumblings Introduction

In the constant struggle to be and stay relevant in the 21st Century dynamic, we run the risk of minimizing the former writ, the Old Testament. It is a daunting task to tell stories from 4000 years ago to people who are addicted to 'Breaking News.' Our audiences are composed of people who check their phones on average 52 times a day to see what's happening now![1] The need for speed often makes the Old Testament seem disconnected from many of today's pressing issues. Yet it is from this ancient book that we hear prophetic rumblings about today's global crisis. From wars and conspiracies to economic disparities, global warming and epidemics, to crime and corruption, it all has been previewed in the Old Testament thousands of years ago.

It is from this platform that Jesus the Christ shared His message of salvation with first century audiences. According to Philip Yancey in his book, "The Bible Jesus Read," He traced in its passages every important fact about himself and his mission. He quoted from it to settle controversies with opponents such as the Pharisees, Sadducees, and Satan himself. The images, Lamb of God, shepherd, sign of Jonah, stone which the builders

---

[1] Deloitte, "Global Mobile Consumer Survey: US Edition 2018," https://www2.deloitte.com/us/en/pages/technology-media-and-telecommunications/articles/global-mobile-consumer-survey-us-edition.html.

rejected, that Jesus used to define Himself came straight from the pages of the Old Testament.[2]

We must continue to preach Christ from the Old Testament to give our audiences a preview of the pain and suffering our Lord endured. Deeper still, the Old Testament points to our ultimate goal, eternal life in paradise with our God. To achieve that end, we are inclined to ponder, where did it all begin?

The sermons in Part One are reflective of challenging questions facing today's believers. In an effort to address uncertainties facing the church (from a pastoral perspective) I draw from the book our Lord used to heal every malady.

In Part One the sermons feature the use of lengthy exposition to set the table for the balance of the sermon. Exposition is a genre in which the purpose is to inform, explain, describe or define. In these four sermons the exposition provides pertinent background information. It gives the history of a pericope of scripture.[3] For exposition to be effective it must be executed early in the sermon. Often the exposition answers five

---

[2] Philip D. Yancey, *The Bible Jesus Read* (Grand Rapids: Zondervan, 1999).

[3] George B. Jackson, *Ordination Training for Bi-vocational Clergy* (Thomasville: Pureheart Publishing Inc., 2017).

questions for the audience. Who? What? When? Where and Why? The exposition takes the listener behind the scene and mentally engages them in the historical event. The social, economic, political and religious protocols of the day are laid bare in the exposition and lay the foundation for a sermon that makes someone in the audience say, "Paint the picture preacher!"

## Who is on the Lord's Side?
### Exodus 32:25-26 RSV

**Text:** *"And when Moses saw that the people had broken loose (for Aaron had let them break loose, to their shame among their enemies), then Moses stood in the gate of the camp, and said, 'Who is on the LORD's side? Come to me.' And all the sons of Levi gathered themselves together to him."*

**Title: Who is on the Lord's Side?**

**Exposition:** Our text today takes us back in time over 3300 years to the year 1300 B.C. Here we witness the meeting between God and Moses on Mount Sinai. Upon Sinai, God issued his laws to Moses; giving the great judge two tables of testimony, tablets of stone, written with the magnificent finger of God. The tablets were inscribed with the 10 commandments for Israel to obey. Moses led Israel out of Egypt under the guidance of Jehovah and the nation was headed for the Promised Land. Up to this point, Israel had showed herself very favorable in her obedience to God. But for some reason (maybe it was immaturity, impatience, or infidelity) while Moses met with God and tarried on Mount Sinai 40 days, the people went astray. Their patience grew thin. They wanted something physical, a leader or something visible to go before them. There is an old saying: I've got to see it to believe it! The high priest Aaron had to make them a god that they could see and follow and control. We want

6

to characterize God. We give God anthropomorphic projections. We want to make God look like and act like us. They wanted the convenience of God without the chastisement of God. Aaron (being as weak as he was) agreed to this sin and he instructed the men and women, boys and girls to take off their golden earrings (yes, even the men and boys wore earrings) and he would make them a god. Then Aaron became a goldsmith and fashioned the melted gold into a calf. Israel suddenly developed convenient amnesia, for they said, "These are our gods, which brought us out of the land of Egypt."

They forgot who brought the plagues on Egypt. They forgot who forced Pharaoh to let Israel go. They forgot who parted the waters and drowned the Egyptian army. They forgot who sent bread from heaven and who provided a pillar of fire by night and a cloud by day. They overlooked who brought water from the rock. They forgot Yahweh's kindness, mercy and longsuffering towards them. We too are guilty of convenient amnesia. Some people rather worship a statue or a thing even now. We conveniently forget past victories in the face of pending defeat. Some people would worship a dead thing; a building or monument or a document rather than worship the true and living God.

The next morning they rose early and had a great feast to honor the lifeless golden calf, an Egyptian symbol of fertility. They drank and partied and had wild orgies all day long to celebrate the day of the golden calf. But God who is omniscient (all seeing and all knowing), saw the mischief of Israel. He told Moses to hurry and get down the mountain for the people had made an idol and sinned against Him. God became angry at Israel and was about to wipe out the entire Israeli nation, when Moses reminded God of His great promises to Abraham, Isaac and Jacob to multiply their seed like the stars in heaven.

**Introduction:** When we pray, we too should use scripture to claim blessings. Jesus Christ said, "Ask and it shall be given, seek and ye shall find, knock and the door will be opened to you," (Matthew 7:7). Remind God that He promised never to leave us nor forsake us. He promised to pour out blessings if we faithfully tithe. He promised to show us His salvation if we would be still. We must be determined to stand on the promises of God.

God decided not to destroy Israel and he hastened Moses to hurry down the mountain and confront the people. Moses descended down the mountain with the two stone tablets. As he approached the camp, Joshua his faithful lieutenant, heard the celebration and thought that a victory party for the Israeli army was going on. But Moses said, "It's not that kind of party!" He saw the calf and the frolic and he broke the tablets at the foot of Sinai, symbolizing the breach of the covenant with God by the nation of Israel. He burned the calf to ashes and mixed the ashes in water and made the children of Israel drink the bitter liquid.

Sometimes when we go astray, we have to swallow our own medicine.

Moses looked to Aaron for an explanation but his brother and his second in command could only plead innocent and blame the people who were "set on mischief." Moses looked on the shame of the people who were still naked from the wild orgy and he issued a question that rings and roars across the sands of time …

**Who is on the Lord's Side?**

I.  I must ask this question because many of us are like the children of Israel. We require physical Gods. A God we can touch and see and manipulate. Some people treat their homes, families, money, jobs, cars and education like their god. Some people worship these things because they don't know whose side they are on. They take for granted that, "Every good gift and every perfect gift is from above," (James 1:17).

   1.  We must be ever mindful that the Lord giveth and the Lord taketh away; blessed be the name of the Lord (Job1:21). Worshipping temporary, physical things will lead to ultimate destruction. Exodus 20:5 says, "I the Lord thy God am a jealous God, visiting the iniquity of the father of the children, unto the third and fourth generations of them that hate me."

9

2. Jesus Christ said, "Thou shalt worship the Lord thy God and Him only shall thou serve," (Luke 4:8). Unlike Satan's do nothing gods, our God is a spirit and they that worship Him must worship Him in spirit and in truth (John 4:24) … **Who is on the Lord's Side?**

II. God wants you to choose whose team you are going to sign up with today. You cannot play for the Eagles and the Rams. You cannot play for the Patriots and the Panthers.

1. You cannot be on two teams at one time. Jesus said, "Thou cannot serve two masters. For you will love the one and hate the other or you will cling to the one and despise the other; you cannot serve God and mammon," (Matthew 6:24).

2. In sports, opposing teams wear different uniforms for identification purposes. Our uniform is the whole armor of God! Will you gird your loins with truth and put on the breast plate of righteousness? Will you cover your feet with the preparation of the gospel of peace and grab the shield of faith to block the enemy's darts? Make sure you put on the helmet of salvation and don't forget the sword of the spirit which is the word of God. Or, will you cloak yourself in half-truths, whole lies and deception?

3. There can be no neutrality. I have not made up my mind yet, won't work in this situation. I am waiting for the

right time is a cop-out. I got to see what's going to happen is an excuse.

4. There will be no fence straddlers. Playing both sides to see who will win is evidence of lack of commitment.

5. Either be for God and against Satan

6. For right and against wrong

7. For love and against hate

8. For truth and against lies

9. For justice and against oppression

10. For Christ and against transgression

11. For the Holy Ghost and against demons

12. Be hot or cold not "lukewarm." Jesus told the church at Laodicea, "I will spew thee out of my mouth," (Revelation 3:16).

III. God wants more players on his team; the roster is not full yet.

1. God accepts all comers (rich, poor, black, white, weary and wretched).

2. The harvest is plentiful, but the laborers are few.

3. To make the team Paul said to, "Confess with your mouth the Lord Jesus Christ and believe in thy human heart that God has raised him from the dead, thou shalt be saved," (Romans 10:9).

4. Jesus Christ said, "If any man would come after Me, let him deny himself daily, take up his cross and follow Me," (Luke 9:23).

**Conclusion**: Like the Levites who joined forces with Moses and stood on the Lord's side, I want to be on a winning team, a team that cannot lose. A team owned by God, managed by Jesus Christ, and coached by the Holy Spirit. Will you join our team?

I'm proud to boast that we have a near perfect record. After a disappointing loss at the beginning of the season in the Garden of Eden, we won a great victory on Noah's Ark. Moses led the team in tackles when we defeated Pharaoh's Army at the Red Sea. Joshua ran the opening kickoff back at Jericho. Daniel sacked all the lions in the lion's den. Elijah caught a long touchdown pass at the River Kishon. Shadrach, Meshach and Abednego blocked a punt in a fiery furnace. Then David kicked a game-winning field goal with time running out in the valley of the shadow of death.

But our greatest triumph was on a hill outside of Jerusalem called Calvary. We were an underdog headed into overtime on the enemy's home field. The score was tied at 39 stripes. Our quarterback had been sacked by the sins of the world. He lay injured on the field. He had been bruised for our iniquities. The chastisement of our peace was upon Him. The enemy drove nails in His hands and feet. For a helmet he wore a crown of thorns. They hit Him so hard; He was bleeding from His side.

The instant replay revealed that the rocks cracked open. Further review showed that the earth shook and the curtain in the temple was rent in two. Our quarterback hung his head and died at 3 p.m. God called a three-day time out and Nicodemus and Josephus of Arimathea carried Him to the locker room to regroup.

Early Sunday morning our Superstar sat up and said, "I'm ready to go back in the game." He walked through hell. He blocked death and the grave. Jesus sacked Satan in the end zone so hard he fumbled the ball and the Lord recovered it for the winning score. He is the MVP of all time! Now he has all power in his hands. God took him out the game forty days later and signed a free-agent named the Holy Ghost on the day of Pentecost.

When you are on the Lord's side, you are more than a conqueror through Him that loved us. When you are on the Lord's side, He will prepare a table before you in the presence of your enemies. When you are on the Lord's side, no weapon formed against you shall prosper. When you are on the Lord's side, "What the enemy meant for evil, the Lord meant it for good to save much people alive," (Genesis 50:20). Joshua declared, "Choose you this day whom ye will serve, whether the gods your fathers served beyond the Jordan or the gods of the Amorites in whose land ye dwell, but as for me and my house we will serve the Lord," (Joshua 24:15)!

With all my heart, all my mind, and all my soul I'm on the Lord's side. If you are on the Lord's side, you ought to stand up and tell the world, "For God I live and for God I will die. Blessed be the name of the Lord." All of my life, I will wait on the Lord until my change comes. For if God be for me, who can be against me … No enemy shall prevail, no weapon shall prosper. No fear shall conquer me. No hell hound shall consume me because I made up my mind; **I'm on the Lord's side**!

# When Dogs Come to Church
## Psalms 22:16 NRSV

**Text**: Yes, dogs are round about me; a company of evildoers encircle me; they have pierced my hands and feet

**Title: When Dogs Come to Church**

**Exposition:** King David, that great monarch of Israel a man after God's own heart, often found himself under attack from his enemies. One in particular was Saul, the first anointed King of Israel. He was jealous of the fighting skill and popular acclaim that his young lieutenant enjoyed. He knew that the people loved David and that God's favor was with him. Saul's fear and envy of David became so intense that he sought to kill him. It was at these times that this anointed King found comfort and solace in Psalms or songs that he would write to express his sorrow, fear and anxiety.

In this song designated to be put to music by the chief musician Ai-je-leth Shahar, David is seriously ill. To make him feel even worse, his enemies have declared that his sickness is a sign that God has abandoned him. They mock him, they laugh at him and ridicule him. The young king is so sick that his neighbors and relatives have begun dividing his property. All he can do in his deteriorated condition is complain, much like our crucified Christ would later lament, "My God, My God why hast thou forsaken me," (Matthew 27:46)? His enemies in joyful anticipation of David being totally consumed by death behave like the bulls of Bashan, snorting, rumbling, roaring and being savages. In this desperate, lonely hour David found himself void of earthly allies. He called on the Lord God Jehovah for healing and deliverance from slanderers. He could no longer hold out. He desperately needed help from His creator.

David was steadfast in his faith. He knew that God would never leave him nor forsake him. The prophet in his lamentation spoke vicariously and prophetically of the suffering of Jesus Christ in his own time of sorrow. Like Jesus, David observed that he was surrounded by those who wanted to see him dead. His enemies were like executioners, waiting to pierce his hands and feet if that would cause him more pain. They were all about him, ready to devour him, like wild dogs when the smell of blood is in the air.

**Introduction:** It is safe to say that where ever you find man, you find dogs. They are one of mankind's oldest and most consistent companions. In all cultures throughout the world, dogs thrive. Carnivores or meat eaters, they have been called man's best friends. Remnants of rock that formed walls of stone age caves picture man and dogs together on what seem to be hunting expeditions. Early man probably bred and trained the first dogs to hunt for food. Later dogs were used for protection from wild animals and other predators. Dogs over the centuries have been a companion to mankind. Yet, while they are a part of our everyday lives (if you don't own one, you certainly know someone who does) there are some areas that are usually off limits to dogs. Places like work, school, hospitals and of course the church. By their nature alone, dogs can be very disruptive, distracting and divisive. Therefore, it is always alarming and problematic, when dogs come to church!

**Definition:** The term *dog* is found in the Bible in both the Old and the New Testaments dozens of times. In the Old Testament, dog comes from the Hebrew word (*Keh-leb*) meaning to attack, or a foreigner or gentile. In the Greek tongue the word for dog is (*koo-ohn*). In Matthew 7:6, Jesus Christ said, "It is not good for us to give that which is holy unto dogs, for they would trample that which is holy under their feet and then turn around and bite you." Dogs, no matter how well trained can be unpredictable, unruly as well as ungrateful at times.

**Definition:** Webster says that not only is a dog a, "Flesh-eating domestic animal related to wolves," but a dog is also described as a worthless fellow. One of the Old Testament definitions for (*keh-leb*) or dog is a male prostitute. Women over the centuries have been very accurate in calling promiscuous men, dogs.

While the term dog describes our beloved house pets, yet the word 'dog' carries negative connotations within its context. Let's look at the record. When someone is expected to lose we call him the underdog. When someone undeserving wins the prize we often comment, "Every dog has his day." When something has gone to the dogs, it is ruined, worthless, and undesirable. When someone dogs you they pursue you, track you down, stalk you and worry you to your wits end. When a person says she's been dogged, we can generally ascertain that she has been mistreated by the man she trusted. When disgusted, many people will say "Well I'll be dog gone!" And when you find yourself in the dog house, you are guilty of doing something you had no business doing.

I. That's why it's always chaotic when dogs come to church. Regardless of how helpful and useful they are in the world they have no place in the house of God. Still, we bring the dog with us to church on Sunday in our attitudes toward one another, in the way we conduct ourselves and in our perception of one another. Maybe this was the source of David's complaint, "Dogs are all around me", barking, moaning, howling, and sniffing. There all kinds of dogs that visit the church, from beagles to cocker spaniels, greyhounds, to common mutts.

1. Sporting or Hound Dogs: These dogs point and pick up a trail. They come looking for trouble. They come in sniffing and scratching around, trying to find something wrong. They persist. No matter how many souls are being saved, no matter how much progress is being made they keep hunting until they find something wrong. It might be something that no one else notices or even cares

18

about but just let the hound dog pick up the scent and it's off to the races. Running across fields and streams, pastures and forest, over hills and down in the valley. Expending great amounts of energy. Dragging everyone with them on the chase, looking for that prized problem. And when the hound finally corners his prey he lets you know. He stops and points and barks as loud as he can for you to come see what he has found. You run to see the prized deer, only to find a possum stuck up a tree. Sporting dogs sometimes imitate people, they look for trouble just for the sport of it all. They love drama so they constantly keep trouble brewing.

2. Then you have your work dogs, Boxers, Collies, Doberman Pinscher, German Shepherd, Rottweiler and St. Bernard. Highly intelligent, agile, strong dogs. These dogs can get the job done. These are big dogs bred to be helpers. They usually carry out their duties well. But work dogs can be loud. Their barks can disrupt and scare people away. Big dogs guard the gate and won't let anybody in. There are people outside today, afraid to come in the church because of big dogs at the gate. I've been told by people who own such animals, "Don't be afraid, he won't bite." My reply is, "Does he have teeth?" If the answer is yes, then I know he will bite, just give him a chance. That's the problem with Dobermans and

Rottweilers and Germans Shepherds. They are so big and reputed to be so mean and bark with such evil intent that the average person won't go near one. Visitors to the church always tense up when a big dog asks, "Where do you come from? Where do you work? Who told you about this church? Why do you want to join this church? Do you know what you are doing?" Big dogs scare people when they bark out, "I've been here since 19 so and so" … guarding the gate, barking at everyone who walks by, "Don't come in here, keep out!" The dangerous thing about work dogs is that in their paranoia and selfishness they will eventually turn on their master, their trainer, the hand that feeds them. Watch out for work dogs for their true loyalty is to be maintaining the status quo at any cost.

3. Then there are the toy dogs, Chihuahua, Pekinese, Poodle and Terrier. These dogs are sometime called house dogs or lap dogs. Cute little things, their bark is much worse than their bite. They are very inquisitive or shall we say nosey. They stay in somebody else's business all the time. They come to church and run other people down. You've seen these toy dogs in the window barking their heads off from the inside of the house. But if you open the door to let them out in the yard, they refuse to come out. When toy dogs come to church they

don't fight, they just push other folks up to fight. When confronted they run and hide under the couch. They seldom face the people whom they ridicule. They don't get into the heat of the conflict; they stay behind the scene and keep everybody focused on the conflict. When you turn your back, they snap at your heels and when you turn around to kick them, they always dart out of harm's way. Toy Dogs remind me of people. They talk about you behind your back like a savage, but when you confront them to their face with their own words, they suddenly develop convenient amnesia. "I never said anything about you. I don't know what you are talking about. That wasn't me. There must be some mistake. I don't talk about people. I never gossip!"

4. Then there are some dogs which are unclassified. Dogs like the Boston Terrier, Bulldog, Chow, Dalmatian and French Poodle. These dogs have some of the same qualities as the other dogs yet they don't function in the same capacities. Basically they just look good. When they come to church they just look good. When it's time to start service they can't come in on time, no one would see them and they really want to be seen. They thrive on attention. They love to have their egos stroked, petted, brushed, and rubbed down. They get offended when overlooked and love to hear their names announced in

public. But, when it's time to roll up our sleeves and break a sweat, they can't be found. They are quick to point out their jam packed schedule, full of important meetings with important people. You know all the dog shows that they must attend and participate in. When it's time to do more than sit around and profile, you can't find them. They are the masters of excuse-ology, "I'm too busy, I'm going out of town. I've got to work. Family emergency, not interested, I've never done that, why can't you get someone else, I'm tired." When it's time to be about the masters business, remember that basically unclassified dogs don't commit to anything. They just want to look good.

II. In Matthew 15:26, Jesus Christ said, "It is not acceptable to take the children's bread and give it to dogs." In this statement or reply to the Syrophoenician woman, Jesus Christ was critical of dogs because of the nature of dogs and the problems associated with dogs.

1. Dogs take a multitude of problems with them everywhere they go. Pest such as fleas, ticks, heartworms, lice and mange. All types of parasite that feed on the health and strength of the animal breaking him down, making him weak, depleting his will.

2. We bring all types of parasites with us to church. Parasites like contempt, which eats away at our souls.

Doubt that makes us question that which surpasses all understanding. Greed, that makes us think only of fulfilling our own selfish desires. Lust, that makes us want that which belongs to someone else. Jealously, that makes us constantly compare ourselves to others. Pride, that makes us think that we are more than we actually are. Fear, which constantly has us, looking over our shoulders, wondering what's around the corner. Complacency, that laissez-faire attitude that makes us satisfied with second best, taking whatever comes as inevitable, making no strides to improve our lot in life.

3. Dogs also possess special hearing abilities. Because of their keen sense of sound, dogs can hear noises at audio levels that most people cannot hear. We have people in the church like that. They can hear things that other folks can't hear. They hear things that seem only a dog could detect. Well I heard that... Rumor has it that... Somebody told me... A reliable source said... I don't want to call any names, but I heard... I promised not to say who told me but...

4. Of course dogs are also characterized by their tendency to dig things up. We do that too! We do all we can to dig up something on somebody else. We will get down low to the ground, until we can sniff out someone's trail. And then we follow the trail as far as we can go. As if

we don't have enough bones in our own back yards, we'll go dig up somebody else's past and say, "Ah-ha. I told you. Look! Well you know he used to go with so and so! She used to be on drugs. He was an alcoholic. Didn't she go to jail? I saw him at the club." Dogs round about, piercing people's hands and feet, digging up old bones. Constantly trying to find something or someone to chew on. Trying to crucify and condemn. Yet Paul said, "All have sinned and fall short of the glory of God," (Romans3:23).

**Conclusion:** I'm glad that when dogs get loose in the church and start barking and growling and creating chaos, I know who to call. I know how to get in touch with the Chief dog catcher. When dogs come to church hungry, ready to devour my very soul I know how to contact the Captain of animal control. When the hounds of hell sniff out my trail and snap at my feet, I know where my help comes from. I know who will, "Deliver my soul from the sword and my life from the power of the dog," (Psalm 22:20). I know that, "Whatever I bind on earth shall be bound in heaven and whatever I loose on earth shall be loose in heaven," (Matthew 18:18).

I know where my hope is built. I know where to place my confidence. When the mongrels attack, I'll pray with David, "Show thy marvelous loving kindness, O thou that savest by thy right hand them which put their trust in thee, from those that rise up against them. Keep me as the apple of thine eye; hide me under the shadow of thy wings," (Psalm 17:7-8). "Defend me from mine enemies, O my God; defend me from them that rise up against me," (Psalm 59:1). "Order my steps in your Word and let not any iniquity have dominion over me," (Psalm 119:133).

When dogs are all around me, I find peace when I hear the poet say, "I've seen the lightning flashing, heard the thunder roll. Felt sins breakers dashing trying to conquer my soul; I heard the voice of Jesus, He bid me still fight on, He promised never to leave me, never to leave me alone.[4]

---

[4] Never Alone, 119 Hymnals, https://hymnary.org/text/ive_seen_the_lightning_flashing.

## You Are In His Will
## Jeremiah 29:11 NIV

**Text:** "For I know the plans I have for you, declares the LORD, plans to prosper you and not to harm you, plans to give you hope and a future."

**Exposition:** From the ancient city of Anathoth, north-east of Jerusalem came a great child prodigy. He was anointed from heaven while still in his mother's womb to preach and prophesy to Israel. His name means, the Lord (*Yahweh*) exalts. In the Hebrew tongue his name is *Yirme Yahu*. We know him as Jeremiah the weeping prophet who lamented over the sins of Judah. The prophet dictated oracles to his aide/secretary Baruch over a span of 47 years from 627-580 B.C. encompassing the reigns of kings Josiah, Jehoiakim, and Zedekiah.

The 29th chapter contains a letter Jeremiah is instructed to send from Jerusalem to the exiled leadership and the people who had been carried away captives to Babylon by King Nebuchadnezzar. Though Jeremiah is dictating the letter to his faithful scribe Baruch, God is dictating to the prophet and the messages sent to encourage and sustain Judah during their 70 years captivity.

I. In verses 5 – 7 the Lord sent Israel a message of defiant optimism.

*"Build houses and settle down; plant gardens and eat what they produce. Marry and have sons and daughters; find wives for your sons and give your daughters in marriage, so that they too may have sons and daughters. Increase in number there; do not decrease. Also, seek the peace and prosperity of the city to which I have carried you into exile. Pray to the LORD for it, because if it prospers, you too will prosper."* He encourages them to bloom where you're planted.

1. As believers we must make the best out of a bad situation. We only have a limited time on this earth, so make every moment count. You might not be where you want to be right now, but do all you can to make your surroundings better.

2. Don't get bogged down in self-deprecation or pity parties. Find a reason to give thanks in your sorrow. Remember the blessings you have previously enjoyed and remind yourself that God is still in the blessing business.

3. Yes, it is bad but it could be worse! You are still alive. You can still pray. You can still smile even when times get hard.

4. When life gives you lemons, learn to make lemonade. Stop complaining, get busy. Push yourself and don't wallow in your mess, get up and move like somebody. Paul declared in (Romans 8:18), "For I consider that the sufferings of this present time are not worthy to be compared with the glory which shall be revealed in us."

II. You can't believe everything you hear from the government, the press, social media, friends or the streets. The prophet in verses 8-11 reports:

*⁸Yes, this is what the LORD Almighty, the God of Israel, says: "Do not let the prophets and diviners among you deceive you. Do not listen to the dreams you encourage them to have. ⁹ They are prophesying lies to you in my name. I have not sent them," declares the LORD. ¹⁰ This is what the LORD says: "When seventy years are completed for Babylon, I will come to you and fulfill my good promise to bring you back to this place.*

1. Consider the source of information. Some folks manipulate information to serve their ulterior motives and keep unnecessary drama going.

2. If you're doing jacked up stuff and your companion is doing jacked up stuff, they have no credentials to advise you. They are false prophets, hustlers, fake counselors, tricksters and liars.

3. Tell the "If I were you" crowd to look in the mirror and get your own raggedy house in order.

4. Please guard your heart. Be careful about sharing your dream or who you articulate your dreams and visions to. Some folks who laugh and smile with you are jealous of your audacity to want more in a time of lack.

III. Remember that even you are in His will!

1. God has plans for you that only God knows. His plans cannot be sabotaged. His plans are written in the Lambs book of life. A book where believers names are written in the blood of our Savior.

2. You don't have to sit in the lawyer's office on pins and needles wondering if God remembered you in His will. He wrote your name in His will from the foundations of the world. You did nothing and there is nothing you could do to be included. For it is by grace you have been saved, through faith and this not of yourselves. It is the gift of God, not by works so no one can boast (Ephesians 2:8-9).

3. His plan may not be clear to us yet. We may be unclear about exactly what we are supposed to be doing. In our confusion we get frustrated but remember, "My thoughts are not your thoughts and my ways are not your ways, says the Lord," (Isaiah 55:8).

4. The plans He has for you are good! Blessed be the Lord, who daily loads us with benefits, the God of our salvation (Psalm 68:19). Oh, give thanks unto the Lord for He is good! For His mercy endures forever (Psalm 118:1). Solomon reported, "The blessings of the Lord makes rich and adds no sorrow," (Proverbs 10:22).

IV. He has already planned your destiny, not your disaster! In 2 Samuel 22:49, David declares "He delivers me from my enemies. You also lift me up above those who rise against me; You have delivered me from the violent man."

1.  Why does he do this? To give us destiny, joy, health, prosperity and strength. Jesus is our future! In John 11:25 our Lord said, "I am the resurrection and the life."

2.  You can now live a victorious, fearless life! Christ encouraged us in John 14:1-3, "Let not your hearts be troubled: ye believe in God believe also in me. In my Father's house are many mansions. I go to prepare a place for you."

**Transition:** Your future will have no lack of resources. The Master declared, "The thief does not come except to steal, and to kill, and destroy. I have come that they might have life, and that they might have it more abundantly," (John 10:10).

**Conclusion:** God promised us a hope - not just any hope. Real hope, not like the world. We hope the x-ray comes back negative. We hope for rain. We hope to win the lottery. We hope for a return call from a job interview. We hope to see you soon. We hope you can make it. We hope there's enough money in the account to cover that check.

But in Christ we don't have just any hope. We have an enduring hope! We have the hope of Earth and the joy of Heaven. We have a hope that says, "Come ye blessed of my

Father and inherit the kingdom prepared for you from the foundations of the world," (Matthew 25:34).

We have hope that says, "And if you be Christ's then you are Abraham's seed and heirs according to the promise," (Galatians 3:29). Our hope says, "And if children then heirs, heirs of God and joint heirs with Christ, if indeed we suffer with Him, that we may also be glorified together," (Romans 8:17). Our hope is worth waiting for! Together we are, "Looking for the blessed hope and glorious appearing of our great God." Edward Mote summed it up in 1834, when he wrote: "My hope is built on nothing less, than Jesus blood and righteousness; I dare not trust the sweetest frame, but wholly lean on Jesus' name. On Christ the solid rock I stand, all other ground is sinking sand."[5]

---

[5] Edward Mote, "My Hope is Built on Nothing Less," https://www.hymnal.net/en/hymn/h/298.

# The Handwriting is on the Wall

## Daniel 5:1-5; 8-9 NKJV

**Text:** *"Belshazzar the king made a great feast for a thousand of his lords and drank wine in the presence of the thousand. While he tasted the wine, Belshazzar gave the command to bring the gold and silver vessels which his father Nebuchadnezzar had taken from the temple which had been in Jerusalem that the king and his lords, his wives, and his concubines might drink from them. Then they brought the gold vessels that had been taken from the temple of the house of God which had been in Jerusalem; and the king and his lords, his wives, and his concubines drank from them. They drank wine, and praised the gods of gold and silver, bronze and iron, wood and stone. In the same hour the fingers of a man's hand appeared and wrote opposite the lampstand on the plaster of the wall of the king's palace; and the king saw the part of the hand that wrote. Now all the king's wise men came, but they could not read the writing, or make known to the king its interpretation. Then King Belshazzar was greatly troubled, his countenance was changed, and his lords were astonished."*

**Title: The Handwriting is on the Wall**

**Exposition:** One of five Major Prophets of the Hebrew Bible is Daniel. A humble prophet of the tribe of Judah, Daniel was a key figure during the 70 years of Israel's captivity in Babylon serving in the courts of Nebuchadnezzar, Nabonidus, Evil-merodach,

32

Belshazzar, Darius and Cyrus. In the year 539 B.C., Belshazzar, the grandson of Nebuchadnezzar reigned over the province of Babylon. A very extravagant and wasteful administrator, the king was noted for throwing wild parties and drinking openly in front of his subject people.

At this great feast noted in our text, Belshazzar is up to his old tricks and in his drunken condition he commits an act of treason or sacrilege against God by telling his servants to bring him the holy drinking goblets that were stolen from the house of God in Jerusalem, by his grandfather Nebuchadnezzar. And so, like Epiphanies before him, Belshazzar and his lords drank wine from the holy vessels and praised and lamented their pagan gods.

It is here that the Lord steps in and begins to write a message on the palace wall. Belshazzar was immediately sober from his drunken condition and the scripture says that his knees knocked, and his legs buckled when he saw this mysterious hand begin to write a message on the palace wall. In great fear the king cried out for his wise men, soothsayers, root doctors, magicians and astrologers to come to the palace and interpret what the message on the wall read. They all tried but no one knew what the message meant, and the king was that much more afraid and bewildered. Over hearing the great commotion, the queen mother approached the throne. She told Belshazzar that there was a man in the province that served in the courts of previous kings, who was wise and gifted in interpreting dreams and mysteries because of his divine spirit. She called him

Belteshazzar as he was named by king Nebuchadnezzar. The Hebrews called him Daniel. Belshazzar summoned the prophet and told him that he would give him a purple robe, a gold chain and the rank of third in authority in Babylon if Daniel would interpret the mysterious writing. Daniel told the king to keep his gifts or give then to someone else. Daniel then told the king what he did not want to hear.

Daniel explained that Nebuchadnezzar; Belshazzar's grandfather had received great favor from God. The Lord had protected him from enemies and spared his allies. The entire world knew and feared Nebuchadnezzar for God was with him. But then one day Nebuchadnezzar became arrogant and puffed up, so much so that he did not honor God.

The Lord had to cut Nebuchadnezzar down and drove him out into the wilderness where he behaved like an animal and grazed among the cattle until he learned who was God and who was subject to God's authority. Daniel told the young king, now you knew all this that happened to your grandfather, and yet you still willingly disrespected God. You knew the Lord's power and yet you still refused to humble yourself and submit to His will. You worshipped idol gods, but the God of heaven, who holds your very breath in his hand, has seen it all, and when you drank wine and made a toast to your idol images from the sacred vessels of the house of God, He had finally seen enough.

**Exegesis:** Now this is the message to you from heaven; Mene, Mene, Tekel, Upharsin.

**Mene:** God has numbered the days of your reign and brought it to an end.

**Tekel:** You have been weighed on the scales and found lacking.

**Upharsin or Peres:** Your kingdom is divided and given to the Medians and Persians. Then as he promised, Belshazzar made Daniel third ruler over the nation. According to the prophecy of the writing on the wall, Belshazzar was assassinated that very night and his kingdom fell into the hands of Darius the Median.

**Title: The Handwriting is on the Wall**

**Introduction:** This morning when I think of America, I think of this great biblical jewel. Belshazzar represents America in all her vile corrupt profligate habits. Daniel represents the Church of the living God, trying to warn this nation that the signs of the times are abundantly clear.

I.   As we conclude the second decade of the 21$^{st}$ Century, it becomes more and more evident that God is sending us unequivocal messages.

   1. War is raging in many different nations simultaneously. Every day we hear about a new crisis. The Rainforest in Brazil are burning at an alarming rate. The average temperature of our earth has increased one degree per year since 2010. Polar icebergs are melting at such a

speedy pace that ocean levels worldwide are increasing two-and one-half inches every 20 years.

2. The world economy is on a seesaw. People struggle from day to day to feed their families and keep a roof over their heads. The value of currency in some nations is almost meaningless. Unemployment figures are low in the U.S., but even those figures fail to reflect those who are being kicked off food stamps, welfare, and needed social benefits. Layoffs have become a part of our everyday lives as plants shut down without warning workers or preparing them for career changes. The minimum wage is stagnant while the cost of living is ever increasing.

3. Disease is rampant in a nation that boasts of having the most advanced health care system on earth. Various mutated forms of cancer and once eradicated viruses will, at some point in the next decade, knock on every door and shake every community because...

**Title: The Handwriting is on the Wall**

4. Crime has made its way from every city street to every country road. It doesn't matter how many security systems or security guards you employ, no office is safe, no home is secure, no car is vandal proof, no church is burglar proof and no computer is hack proof.

5. Murder is a common occurrence. People kill one another as if it were a sport. Black folks are killing black folks as if we are

living in the wild, Wild West. If we are not blowing one another's brains out, the police are doing it for us. We hate one another more efficiently than anyone else could ever hate us. Black folks are about to run the KKK out of business, all the while white nationalist are making domestic terrorism the order of the day.

6. Drug abuse, like the devil himself will not go away. Its big business, its high profile, its power and politics, and its control and genocide. It's more than a junkie on the streets, more than a dealer in the crack house; it's beyond the local distribution level. It's the starch pressed collars sitting behind the desk of some of Americas leading pharmaceutical corporations laughing all the way to the bank, taking no responsibility for the opioid crisis they sponsored.

7. Churches have become more like battlefields than holy grounds. So called Christians come to the house of prayer with plots and schemes and words of division. The saints some time more resemble haints. I love you has been replaced with he makes me sick. She ain't all she says she is. Officers rebel and oppose the pastor. Relatives enter the sanctuary and do not even speak to one another. We have allowed money to become more important than the salvation of the lost and the empowerment of the weak and oppressed.

**Title: The Handwriting is on the Wall**

II.   And just like Belshazzar who would not listen or take heed to what the Lord told him in the life of his grandfather Nebuchadnezzar, America has also been warned time and time again to repent and seek the Lord, but she will not listen.

1.   When someone will not hear what you are saying, it serves the purpose to write it down. That's why the Lord said, "Write the vision and make it plain upon tables that he may run that reads it. For the vision is yet for an appointed time, but at the end it shall speak, and not lie though it tarry wait for it; because it will surely come, it will not tarry," (Habakkuk 2:3).

2.   I can see God writing on the wall of our existence. We must open our receptors and embrace His command.

3.   The message is clear and evident to see. Ignoring the message will not make it go away.

4.   The world is turning upside down. This world is flipping backside over. The world is turning inside out.

5.   I believe that God has just about seen enough of our   self-indulgent foolishness. You may be able to rationalize and fantasize your way into your own facsimile of heaven on earth. But the God I serve is no dummy and he won't be fooled by our trickery.  The Apostle Paul wrote, "Be not deceived; God is not mocked: for whatsoever a man soweth, that shall he also reap," (Galatians 6:7). God is trying to tell

you something today. Martin Luther King Jr. tried to warn us 50 years ago. America's perverted drum major instinct is a prescription for eminent doom. [6]

6. This country is on a collision course with destruction! The wrath of God is upon this nation for how we have mistreated the foreigner and immigrant at the Southern border. "For the Lord thy God is a jealous God, visiting the iniquity of the fathers upon the children unto the third and fourth generation of them that hate me," (Exodus 20:5).

**Title: The Handwriting is on the Wall**

III. In my mind I can hear God saying to this nation:

1. I sent a flood in the days of Noah; they would not hear me...

2. I sent fire and brimstone at Sodom and Gomorrah; still they would not hear me...

3. I sent my prophets, they declared my word, and they would not hear me. They slay and persecuted each one.

4. I sent my only begotten son, the Lamb of God to save the world. Those to whom He was sent to save abused Him, persecuted Him, accused Him, crucified Him on that rugged cross and buried Him in a borrowed grave. Yet, I loved you so much that I woke Him up on the third day

---

[6] Martin Luther King, Jr., "The Drum Major Instinct," Sermon Delivered at Ebenezer Baptist Church, (Atlanta, 1968).

morning with all power in His hand, and you still refused to listen.

5. They killed all my apostles, James and Stephen, Peter and Paul.

6. I kept trying to reach you, but you would not listen. Look at what you did to Lincoln, Nat Turner, John Brown, Marcus Garvey, Malcolm X, Medgar Evers, John Kennedy, Martin Luther King, Jr., and Robert F. Kennedy; you killed them all... the blood is on your hands.

7. I can hear God from upon high. You ask how? Because the spirit of the Lord is upon me, because he hath anointed me to preach the gospel to the poor (Luke 4:18).

**Title: The Handwriting is on the Wall**

8. God is saying, look children, at the signs in the sun and moon and stars. There is great grief and distress among the nations, perplexity and roaring in the sea... Men are fainting with fear in expectation of things that are coming, and the powers of the heavens are shaking uncontrollably.

**Conclusion:** The message on the wall from God is clear. It's the same one John the Baptist gave over 2000 years ago. "Repent for the kingdom of God is at hand," (Mark1:15). Jesus the Christ is on His way soon and very soon with healing in His wings. He's coming in a cloud with power and great glory. He's coming with tens of thousands of His saints to execute judgment upon us all.

When He comes, the Word says, "Every valley shall be exalted, every hill shall be made low, the rough places shall be made smooth and the crooked places shall be made straight and the glory of the Lord shall be revealed, and all flesh shall see it together," (Isaiah 40:4-5).

Then it won't matter who you are or what you believe, every knee shall bow, and every tongue shall confess that Jesus Christ is Lord. Jesus Christ is coming to claim his bride. He is coming with a two-edged sword in His right hand, thunder and lightning in His left hand. Vengeance in His right hand, justice in His left hand. The Sun in His right hand, the moon in His left hand. Eternity in His right hand, infinity in His left hand. Armageddon in His right hand, Apocalypse in His left hand. You better get right with God and do it now, for it is getting late in the evening and the sun is going down.

The handwriting is on the wall. Social unrest every week, murder every day, unpredictable weather patterns, mudslides, tornadoes, heat waves, and raging floods. Doppler radar and meteorologists are baffled. Wars have intensified. The value of human life is at an all-time low. Churches are at odds within themselves, people are fleeing the sanctuary and pouring out into the streets. The environment is poison. The cost of health care is so high, who can afford to be sick. The Lord is trying to tell us something. I believe He is saying,

"If my people, which are called by my name, shall humble themselves and pray, and seek my face, and turn from their wicked ways; then will I hear from heaven, and will forgive their sin, and will heal their land," (2 Chronicles 7:14).

Part Two
The Truth Speaks With Power

## The Truth Speaks With Power Introduction

Lies. Our society is incumbered with lies. Quite frankly, the U.S. was established on the lie of, "Life, liberty and the pursuit of happiness," while simultaneously holding almost four million black slaves at the turn of the 'Civil War.' Lies are dangerous in that they must be covered with more lies until they mount up to become imposing. Jesus approached lies with uncompromising disdain. He told the Pharisees who accused Him of being demon possessed in John chapter eight; "You are from your father the devil, and you choose to do your father's desires. He was a murderer from the beginning and does not stand in the truth, because there is no truth in him. When he lies, he speaks according to his own nature, for he is a liar and the father of lies."

Our Lord is the 'Word' of God. He was in the beginning and He is the final Word. In a world of liars, schemers, deceivers and manipulators, people need the truth. The uncut, unadulterated, unbiased, undeniable truth from our Savior's lips will heal our nation and bring millennials back to our churches.

In Part Two, the sermons are urgent and demanding. The Master calls us to preach in His power and authority. We are challenged and indicted to be passionate and not passive. He told His disciples, "I am the way, the truth and the life, no man cometh unto the Father, but by me," (John 14:6). We must preach this *'truth'* and preach it with the confidence and assurance that the truth shall make you free even in a climate of deception and unabashed corruption.

Part Two features a prevalence of labeling in the manuscript. Labels are like mapping in a sermon document. I think it is essential in the navigation of a sermon to have structure imbedded in the manuscript. Unforeseen events can occur while delivering a sermon. People move, babies scream, doors open, cell phones ring and pages fall from the podium. When the unexpected happens (and it will) the preacher will be distracted and possibly lose her place in the manuscript. When labels are properly inserted throughout the body of the sermon the preacher controls the pace and intensity level of the delivery. Labels help us know what's coming up next in the message and makes transitions smooth. Labels in the sermon include but not limited to; text, title, introduction, exposition, exegesis, definition, major point, subpoint, transition and conclusion (not always in that order).

# We Need Peace
## Matthew 5:9 NIV

**Text:** Blessed are the peacemakers: for they shall be called the children of God.

**Exposition:** In 1491 B.C., Moses received the Ten Commandments from the Lord on Mt. Sinai. This system of laws governs our relationship with God and our fellowship with one another. Our laws today are based upon these Ten Commandments. In the Jewish tradition the penalties were severe for those caught breaking the law. Unfortunately, the Jews often seasoned the law with their own version of justice. There was little mercy. The laws were hard to live under and many people suffered at the hands of misplaced ritualism.

Over 1500 years later a carpenter from Nazareth would issue a new ordinance this time from a mountain in Galilee. He was not there to depreciate the law. He was there to fulfill the law. In fact, He is hope within the law and our only refuge from the brutal sin nature of the law. The Apostle Paul observed, "The sting of death is sin; and the strength of sin is the law. But Thanks be to God, which giveth us the victory through our Lord Jesus Christ," (1 Corinthians 15:56-57).

On this Galilean hill, Jesus revealed the nature of the Kingdom of Heaven and raising the law of Moses to a new level, He also revealed to lost men and women the compassionate, long suffering nature of our omnipotent God. "For, the Law was given through Moses, but grace and truth came through Jesus Christ," (John 1:17). In this historic message which some men have called the epitome or zenith of human expression, Jesus declared a new standard of excellence. He challenged the status quo with revolutionary new concepts. In the Beatitudes, He tells us that the oppressed shall one day overcome their oppressors.

I.   On December 24, 1967, Martin Luther King, Jr. stood before the congregation of Ebenezer Baptist Church in Atlanta, Georgia, and delivered, "A Christmas Sermon on Peace."[7] American troops were in the jungles of Vietnam, fighting an unpopular war against a crafty and elusive enemy. Racial tension was apparent in the summer riots that spread like wildfire in the urban centers of our nation. The campaign for the White House was heating up after President Lyndon B. Johnson announced that he would not seek a second term in office.[8] Consequently, pro-black radicals were mounting an

--------

[7] Martin Luther King, Jr., "A Christmas Sermon on Peace," (Beacon Broadside Press, December 24, 1967), https://www.beaconbroadside.com/broadside/2017/12/martin-luther-king-jrs-christmas-sermon-peace-still-prophetic-50-years-later.html.

[8] Matthew Dallek, "LBJ Announced He Wouldn't Run Again. Political Chaos Ensued," https://www.history.com/news/lbj-exit-1968-presidential-race.

aggressive campaign through groups like the Black Panther Party for Self-Defense to encourage black people to take up arms and abandon non-violence.[9]

1. Against this backdrop of chaos and mayhem, Martin King preached a courageous sermon on a forgotten subject: Peace. Dr. King said, "We have experimented with the meaning of nonviolence in our struggle for racial justice in the United States, but now the time has come for man to experiment with nonviolence in all areas of human conflict, and that means nonviolence on an international scale."[10]

2. Fifty-two years later King's words must be reassessed. Peace must again become a national priority. Martin argued, "Wisdom, born of experience should tell us that war is obsolete."[11]

II. We must abandon the old Levitical concept of an "eye for an eye, a tooth for a tooth and a life for a life." Jesus knew that violence only produces more violence, that those who live by the sword shall ultimately perish by the same and establish a

---

[9] Dr. Huey P. Newton Foundation, *The Black Panther Party: Service to the People Programs*, ed. David Hilliard (Albuquerque: University of New Mexico Press, 2008).
[10] Martin Luther King, Jr., "Triple Evils," *The King Philosophy*, https://thekingcenter.org/king-philosophy/
[11] Ibid, Martin Luther King, Jr., A Christmas Sermon on Peace.

legacy of destructive aggression. The domestic terrorism we continue to experience at home, at work, at school and in houses of worship, is a reflection of a national obsession with guns. We have equated; "Superpower with firepower."[12] We are so intoxicated with violence that we have concocted the notion that the bullet is more effective than the ballot.

1. Dr. King once said that this means of confrontational conflict resolution would "leave too many people blind and toothless."[13] If we continue to volley evil for evil, we only create a venue for evil to flourish. We cannot live by the dictates of violence because the cost is too great, and the reparations never end but trickle down from generation to generation.

2. Jesus knew that this edict of brotherly love and concern for all mankind would meet with a cold reception. He knew it would be unpopular in the opinion polls, even rejected as treasonous. Yet, He knew he was right. Therefore, He stood against that which was morally wrong. "We should take on the whole armor of God so that we might withstand in the evil day and having done

---

[12] Malcolm Moore, China: A Force Fit For a Superpower, *The Telegraph*, https://www.telegraph.co.uk/news/worldnews/asia/china/8251307/China-a-force-fit-for-a-superpower.html.
[13] Martin Luther King, Jr., "Quotes," https://www.goodreads.com/quotes/56448-if-we-do-an-eye-for-an-eye-and-a.

all to stand," (Ephesians 6:13). Martin Luther King once proclaimed, "The true measure of a man is not where he stands in moments of comfort and convenience, but where he stands at times of challenge and controversy."[14]

3.   In Luke 6:29, Jesus Christ told His disciples to turn the other cheek when struck by or offended by an enemy. He urged them to retaliate with love; to kill them with kindness.

III. After the atrocities of September 11, 2001, the paradigm of violent retribution seems to be a foregone conclusion.

1.   In that America is the last remaining global "super power" the "other cheek" philosophy obviously does not apply to us. "Our scientific power has outrun our spiritual power. We have guided missiles and misguided man."[15]

2.   We lost almost 3,000 people on that fateful day in September and the world saw that we were vulnerable. The sleeping giant has been disturbed from his sleep and all the tea cups in the China shop are in danger.

---

[14] Martin Luther King, Jr., "Champions of Human Rights: Martin Luther King Jr. (1929-1968)," *Voices for Human Rights*, https://www.humanrights.com/voices-for-human-rights/martin-luther-king-jr.html.
   [15] Martin Luther King, Jr., "Martin Luther King, Jr. Quotes," *Brainy Quote*, https://www.brainyquote.com/quotes/martin_luther_king_jr_102371.

3.  There is no doubt in my mind that the terrorist threats of Al Quedda, Osama Bin Laden and Muslim extremist were real. I agree with President Bush that Saddam Hussein was a tyrant, a ruthless dictator, and a rat that needed extermination. But why burn down the whole house to catch one rat?

4.  In our zeal to secure Iraqi Freedom we suffered too many American, Coalition and Iraqi casualties. How many is too many? One! One mother who has to grieve over the mangled body of the fruit of her womb. One wife who must explain to her children (American, British, Afghan, or Iraqi children) that their father is never coming home again. News reporters on the frontlines of battle report the number of KIA (Killed in Action) as if the combatants were toy soldiers. Only 150 Afghans killed, 200 coalition soldiers killed, 1000 Iraqi soldiers dead, 500 civilians lost. This wholesale approach to death is sacrilege. John Donne wrote, "No man is an island entire of himself. Every man is a piece of the continent, a part of the main. Any man's death diminishes me because I am a part of humanity. Therefore, never send to know for whom the bell tolls; it tolls for thee!"[16]

---

[16] John Donne, "John Donne Quotes," Brainy Quote, https://www.brainyquote.com/quotes/john_donne_136861.

IV. Jesus instructed us to be peacemakers. We cannot dismiss His universal command as fairy tale or idle chatter or chronologically irrelevant in a contemporary, wireless, cloud based society.

1. The biblical idea of peacemaking is not merely a call to a truce, but rather to make whole that which had been chaotic, to harmonize jangling discords into fraternal symphony. Satan wants to divide us, keep us off balance, angry and maladjusted, at odds with one another. Paul encourages us, "For as many of you as have been baptized into Christ have put on Christ. There is neither Jew nor Greek, there is neither bond nor free, there is neither male nor female: for ye are all one in Christ Jesus. And if ye be Christ's then are ye Abraham's seed, and heirs according to the promise," (Galatians 3:27-29). The apostle warns us, "Owe no man anything, but to love one another: for he that loveth another hath fulfilled the law," (Romans 13:8).

2. In Luke Chapter 21, Jesus Christ warns of wars and the awful rumors associated with them; civil wars, natural disaster and persecution. Yet, the born again who obediently renders his portion to God and Caesar must stand firm as an instrument of peace.

3. Peacemakers are those who have a peaceful disposition, an affection towards peace, an affinity toward tranquility. The psalmist lamented; "My soul hath long dwelt with him that hateth peace. I am for peace: but when I speak, they are for war," (Psalm 120:6-7).

4. Peacemakers are those who have a peaceable conversation. They strive to preserve the peace to keep it whole and repair it when broken. They respond to proposals of peace and are willing to negotiate with rivals to recover peace.

5. Making peace is often a thankless job. It is often the consequence of one who breaks up a fight to receive undeserved blows from both sides, yet peace is worth the blood, sweat and tears.

6. Jesus Christ said we are "Blessed" (*Makarios)* for making peace. In other words, we are fully satisfied not because of favorable circumstances but because of the indwelling of God in our sanctified souls. This enables us to be in the world and yet independent of the world. In this blessed status we are one with Christ who entered the world to stay all enmities and declare peace on earth, good will toward all men.

**Conclusion:** This war-torn world is devoid of peace. No one among us can make peace. Christ alone is the great peacemaker. He made peace by His blood between a righteous God and unrighteous sinners. "Therefore, being justified by faith we have peace with God through our Lord Jesus Christ," (Romans 5:1).

Being peacemakers entitles us to the status "children of God." Our Father is the God of Peace (Jehovah Shalom). His son appeared in theophany as Melchizedek (King of Peace) and sits on the right hand of the throne of God as the 'Prince of Peace'. The spirit of adoption is the spirit of peace.

Consequently, if the peacemakers are blessed, then the peace-breakers must be cursed! For Christ never intended His gospel to be propagated by fire, sword, law, legislation, bigotry, intolerance, imperialism or materialism. These are cancers to the soul of humanity. The gospel is spread using the fruit of the spirit, love, joy, peace, patience, kindness, goodness, faithfulness, humility and self-control.

Thank you Lord, for a peace that the world cannot give nor take away! A peace that can't be explained or comprehended. Jesus Christ declared, "Peace I leave with you, my peace I give unto you; not as the world giveth, give I unto you. Let not your heart be troubled, neither let it be afraid," (John 14:27).

In the midst of the Trump administrations blatant inhumanity and atrocities against people of color, I'm glad that I know where to find my peace. In the midst of life's vicissitudes I can call on my great Redeemer who will say to the wind and waves; "Peace be still." Jesus is our peace. Having abolished in

His flesh the enmity, contained in ordinances; so making peace," (Psalm 2:14-15).

King David declared, "Though a host should encamp against me, my heart shall not fear: though war should rise against me, in this will I be confident. One thing have I desired of the Lord that will I seek after; that I may dwell in the house of the Lord all the days of my life, to behold the beauty of the Lord, and to inquire in his temple. For in the time of trouble he shall hide me in his pavilion: in the secret of his tabernacle shall he hide me; he shall set me up upon a rock," (Psalms 27:3-5).

When babies are snatched out of the arms of their mothers at the Southern Border, when domestic terrorist shoot up churches, synagogues, and Walmart, when voter suppression is a campaign strategy, I won't fear. I won't throw in the towel, for I have concluded that the battle is not mine, it is the Lord's. I co-sign what Paul said in 2nd Timothy 1:7; "God did not give us a spirit of fear, but the spirit of love, power and a sound mind." I'll maintain my composure because after the long night of tears I know joy will come in the morning.

I agree with Martin King Jr. "I still believe that one day mankind will bow before the alters of God and be crowned triumphant over war and bloodshed, and nonviolent redemptive goodwill will proclaim the rule of the land."[17] "And the peace of God which surpasseth all understanding shall keep your hearts and minds through Christ Jesus," (Philippians 4:7).

---

[17] Martin Luther King, Jr., "Quotes Martin Luther King, Jr.," AZ Quotes, https://www.azquotes.com/quote/757999.

## Undercover Christians
## Mark 8:38 KJV

**Text:** Whosoever therefore shall be ashamed of Me and My words in this adulterous and sinful generation; of him shall the Son of Man be ashamed, when He cometh in the glory of His Father with the Holy angels.

**Title: Undercover Christians**

**Exposition:** Sandwiched between Peter's great confession "Thou art the Christ" and the transfiguration, we observe our Saviors teaching on discipleship. Jesus explains that the cost of following Him includes, ridicule, sufferings, tribulations and self-denial. The time in which He came into the world was a time of political occupation by the Romans. To be subject to anyone other than Caesar was considered treason (grounds for execution). Yet he instructed the multitudes to risk their physical lives and follow Him in order to save their spiritual lives in heaven. Jesus Christ said, "For any man that would save his life would lose it, and any that would lose his life for my sake would gain it," (Matthew 16:25).

**Exegesis:** Our text today challenges us to own Christ for who He is. Some will argue, 'I love Jesus,' yet in front of the world, we will disown Him. We shrink before our witness because we don't want the world (full of viciousness, vanity, adultery and transgression) to know who we are and whose we are. We would rather keep it to ourselves. You know, it's our little secret and nobody needs to know because we're …

**Title: Undercover Christians**

**Introduction:** One of my favorite theater characters has long been James Bond. He's suave, smooth, cool, calm, debonair, sophisticated and magnetic. In his movies he is always given a code name that he operates under, 007.[18] He is often in disguise and incognito. He does not want people to know who he is, it might blow his cover. He must assume other identities in order to conceal his own. While this is expedient for spies, it's the road to ruin for Christians who must let their light shine before men, that God might be glorified in their lives.

**Definition:** Undercover Christians are those who claim that they follow Jesus, but follow Him from a distance, from far off, even in obscurity. They are undercover because they act as if they want to keep their faith a secret. They try to keep their commitment to God on the down low, on the tiptoe. They feel like nobody has to know. They hide behind a cloak of Christian anonymity in order to avoid being pointed out, linked with Jesus and exposed to the world. In other words, they are hypocrites.

---

[18] 007, "Inside the World of James Bond," https://www.007.com/.

I. The first type of undercover Christian is the Secret Agent

1. The primary goal of the secret agent Christian is to find out top secret, sometimes damaging information without getting caught. We have many secret agents in the church today.

2. You can't catch them at Bible Study. That would expose them. Someone might think they love the Lord. Someone might assume that they have been saved. Someone might ask them a question about some aspect of faith and then they might have to come up with an answer.

3. You can't catch them at Sunday School. That's too early. They need to sleep late on Sunday morning. If you see them at Sunday school, you might think they are committed to God. Someone might think they are studying to show themselves approved unto God, a workman that needth not be ashamed rightly dividing the word of truth. If you saw them at Sunday School you might start to believe that they love the word of God and the Lord's gospel. It would look like they were being obedient to the will of the Almighty and that would be a dead giveaway.

4. You won't catch the secret agent at church every Sunday. He may drop in once every few months or so to see what's going on, but the odds of seeing him on a regular

basis are very slim. If he comes too often someone might ask him to join something or do something. Someone might take it that he's dependable. Someone might ask him to participate and be a part of the choir, or ushers or evangelism team. No, coming to church routinely is too risky! His cover could be blown.

5. You won't catch the secret agent Christian tithing. Never. He's got too many spy gadgets to buy with his money. He's not sure what they might do with his money. It's his and he's going to keep it. God has nothing to do with his money. He rationalizes that Jesus never told us to tithe. But remember Jesus was an obedient Jew who never broke a law, commandment or covenant which included tithing. The secret agent gives God a piece of what's left after everybody else gets paid. He assures himself that 'God knows I've got bills, he won't mind being last. I'll make up for it when I get some extra money.' Yeah, right, that's why the secret agent stays broke and often resorts to desperate measures to make ends meet.

6. The secret agent always has to leave early yet he always comes late. He can't make it to meetings, rehearsals or special events. You won't see him at an afternoon or evening service that might make you think he loves the Lord. You might get the wrong idea if he comes to

revival. That would implicate him. People would know whose he is and who he works for and who really pays his bills.

II. The second kind of undercover Christian is the Double Agent.

    1. She's more deadly and covert than the secret agent. The double agent plays both sides of the fence at the same time. She plays the ends against the middle. You don't know whether she's coming or going, for you or against you. Friend or foe. Ally or adversary.

    2. The double agent comes to church regularly, seldom misses a Sunday. She makes an appearance whenever she can.

    3. The double agent makes it to Sunday School and bible study occasionally. Her motive is not to participate, but to do reconnaissance, you know, see what's going on.

    4. She pops up every now and then. She's in the church, but the church is not in her. Her heart is in it, but never completely. She wants to do better, but she's a double agent, a Bernadette Arnold and she can't expose herself.

    5. In the movie *Deep Cover*[19], Lawrence Fishburne played an undercover drug enforcement agent who went behind the

---

[19] Roger Ebert, "Deep Cover," https://www.rogerebert.com/reviews/deep-cover-1992.

lines of a major drug cartel to bring down a kingpin. He had to go deep undercover to get to the root of the drug trade. Along the way he got sucked in so deep that the lines of demarcation were blurred and he was no longer able to distinguish the good guys from the bad. He went so deep that he became part of the problem, rather than part of the solution. James 1:8 warns that, "A double minded man is unstable in all his ways."

6. That's the problem with being a double agent. You get sucked in so deep that you lose your identity. You fall and can't get up. Jesus Christ said, "You cannot serve two masters, for you will love the one and hate the other or you will cling to the one and despise the other. You cannot serve God and mammon," (Matthew 6:24).

7. Double agents live in moral, mental and spiritual decay and conflict. You see, it's hard to work for Christ while slipping in the back door of the local club late at night. It's hard to work for the Lord while running from pillar to post in the wee hours of the morning. It's hard to be a saint on Sunday morning after being a haint the night before. It's Christian treason to hold up the blood-stained banner of Christ while decapitating your brothers and sisters. It's hypocritical to follow Jesus Christ while gossiping about other folks, lying on people and promoting drama. It's hard to be a Christian smiling on

the outside, while inside you're planning to destroy someone's character. You can't play both sides and expect to be in God's favor. You will be sucked in just like Peter was at the Last Supper. Jesus Christ said, "Peter, Satan desires to have you and sift you as wheat," (Luke 22:31).

III. Another danger of being a double agent is that at times you get so caught up in not getting caught, you get so deep under the covers that you end up sleeping with the enemy. For deception and trickery makes strange bed fellows.

1. You give up so much to gain so little. You make silly sacrifices attempting to prove your point. You alienate the people that want to help you with your paranoid self-righteousness.

2. You have to prostitute yourself just to keep up with the status quo. Compromising standards and principles just to feed your greed.

3. You end up laying down your faith or laying down your trust in the Lord, just to get what you want, but you never get what you really need. Your glass always seems half empty. You're momentarily happy, but never content.

4. When you lay down with the enemy you essentially lay down with the adversary just to make yourself look good. Lay down with the deceiver to spite someone else unaware that you've made a fool of yourself. Sleep with

Lucifer to get ahead of everyone else and enjoy the finer things of this world. Surprise! You've been pimped. Jesus Christ asked; "What would it profit a man that he gain the entire world and yet lose his soul or, what can a man give in exchange for his soul," (Mark 8:36).

5.  When you sleep with the enemy you put the world before God, you put yourself before God, you put your greed before God, you put your lusts before God, you go as far as to put your personal ambition before our Father. "But be not dismayed, God is not mocked. Whatsoever a man soweth, that shall he reap," (Galatians 6:7). You gamble and compromise His unconditional love for you. The God I serve will not be second to anything or anyone. "For the Lord thy God is jealous, visiting the iniquities of those who hate Him unto the third and fourth generations," (Exodus 20:5).

**Conclusion:** The Master wants you to come from under the covers. He wants you to stop playing "I Spy".[20] He wants bold saints who are not afraid to stand up and declare, 'For God I live and for God I will die.' God wants soldiers who will; "Be steadfast, unmovable always abounding in the work of the Lord,

---

[20] Roger Ebert, "I Spy," https://www.rogerebert.com/reviews/i-spy-2002.

for as much as ye know that your labor is not in vain in the Lord," (1 Corinthians 15:58).

It's time to pull the sheet back on your testimony. It's time to surrender your cloak and dagger religion. It's time to forget about who's looking. It's time to stop peeking around corners to see if the coast is clear to praise the Lord.

Believer, it's time to come out of the closet. Have you not heard? "There is no secret, what God can do. What he's done for others, He will do the same for you."[21]

Jesus said, "But he who denies me before men will be denied before the angels of God," (Luke 12:9). You can't expect to receive a special welcome in heaven when you treat Jesus like a stranger or the invisible man on earth.

Saints, it's time to strip off the cloak of anonymity and let the world know that you have been born again. Jesus said, "For there is nothing covered, that shall not be revealed; neither hid, that shall not be known," (Luke 12:2).

Paul said, "I am not ashamed of the gospel of Christ: for it is the power of God unto salvation to everyone that believeth; to the Jew first, and also to the Greek," (Romans 1:16).

---

[21] Stuart Hamblen, "Sang by Mahalia Jackson, It Is No Secret What God Can Do," Universal Music Publishing Group, Hamblen Music Company.

I'm glad to proclaim to a lost world, "Oh how I love Jesus because He first loved me."[22] I love Him because He is Wonderful, Counselor, Mighty God, Everlasting Father, Prince of Peace, Good Shepherd, Great I Am, Son of Righteousness with healing in his wings.

I'm proud to tell the world that God saved me! Jesus sanctified me! The Holy Ghost filled me up with fire, from upon high. I'll tell the Muslim, the atheist, the root worker, the Buddhist, the Agnostic and politically correct, I'm on the Lord's side! "For I know, that my redeemer liveth, and that he shall stand at the latter day upon the earth; and though after my skin worms destroy this body, yet in my flesh shall I see God," (Job 19:25-26). I'll tell the world, "He brought me out of darkness into the marvelous light, look where he brought me from."[23]

---

[22] Frederick Whitfield, "Oh How I Love Jesus," *Public Domain*, 1855. https://library.timelesstruths.org/music/Oh_How_I_Love_Jesus/.
[23] Tommy Jones, "Look Where He Brought Me From," http://www.allgospellyrics.com/?sec=listing&lyricid=6717.

## My Words Shall Not Pass Away
### Luke 21:32-33 NIV

**Text:** Verily I say unto you, this generation shall not pass away, till all be fulfilled. Heaven and earth shall pass away: but my words shall not pass away.

**Exposition:** As he approached the end of His ministry on earth in the Spring of 29A.D., Jesus was asked by His disciples what signs they should look for to signal the end of time (as we understand.) This was pertinent to the end of His walk on earth. Therefore Christ gave the subject His full attention. Jesus warned them of a coming anti-Christ, wars and their awful rumors, the rise of nation against nation, civil war, earthquakes, famines, pestilence, religious persecution and imprisonment. Jesus prophesied the downfall of Jerusalem, which transpired some 38 years after His crucifixion by the forces of Rome. He told his disciples to look for signs, in the sun and in the moon and stars, even in the earth. And though all of these frightening things would come to pass and the world as we comprehend it would cease to exist, Jesus reassures us that heaven and earth would pass away, but His eternal words would last forever and ever.

**Title: My Words Shall Not Pass Away**

**Introduction:** Our text today deals closely with the final, climatic days of instruction by Jesus Christ the master teacher. We have no earthly record of His scholastic or academic achievements. We know that His parents fled to Egypt when He was two years old to avoid Herod's wrath.

In Egypt, where the first civilizations evolved, He could possibly have studied medicine for the purpose of healing, from the students of Imhotep (the father of medicine). He could have studied mathematics from the students of Ptahhotep (father of science). But it is not until He was 12 years old that we see Him in the temple asking the learned and great minds of that day questions far beyond His maturity.

For the next 18 years, the pages of the life of Christ are blank. We have no idea what He was doing. We can only speculate that He was growing and maturing and developing and praying and serving His Father. He was preparing to preach and teach the gospel. So now here is Christ, after a decade in Egypt and 18 years in Nazareth, about to conclude three years of public ministry. His life had rushed by Him. His time on earth chronologically was so short. It seems as if the great, giant figures immemorial, instrumental in shaping American history died young. Nat Turner (31 years old), Garvey (52 years old), John F. Kennedy (46 years old), Malcolm X (39 years old),

Martin Luther King, Jr. (39 years old) and Robert Kennedy (42 years old).

Let us look at the God - Man of Galilee, the hope of a dying world, about to assemble His faithful for a last supper. He did not have any money to leave behind. He had no property to bestow. No last will and testament. He had no degree on His office wall. His office was the hedges, the highways and byways. He had no earthly possessions to distribute. All He had was words. His precious, priceless, perfect words.

I.  How often do we hear about a family at odds over how to split the inheritance of a departed loved one? Fighting over jewelry, money, home and property as if these material possessions will afford them a few more precious moments with the deceased person, all to no avail. Jesus announced...

**Title: My Words Shall Not Pass Away**

1.  When He spoke of heaven, Jesus was talking about the stars and the planets, the moon, the sun, and all the interplanetary beings, the components of the galactic Milky Way. Jesus also knew of a heaven that we can only imagine. We fantasize about heaven composed of streets of gold, walls of jasper, rivers flowing with milk and honey, endless anthropomorphic projections of what we think heaven should be. Jesus knew about the third heaven, where Elohim, the maker of worlds, the ruler and preserver of the universe dwells.

70

2. When Jesus spoke of the earth, He was referring to the mountains, valleys, rivers, oceans; everything that makes up the planet. Even the vegetation, animals, marine life and the most precious commodity on the globe, mankind, will ultimately pass away.

3. John the Revelator, on the Island of Patmos declared, "I saw a new heaven and a new earth, for the first heaven and the first earth were passed away and there was no more sea. And I, John, saw a Holy city, New Jerusalem coming down from God out of heaven, adorned as a bride prepared to meet her husband," (Revelation 21:1-2).

4. Man is a finite creature. Our time on earth is very short. We are here, but for a fleeting moment. Unfortunately, time is not our friend but a great indifferent foe. We are but pilgrims passing through a barren land. A poet has said, "I've been living in a strange land, and a mighty long way from home."[24]

5. The things we call permanent, unsinkable and super durable, God calls fleeting, fragile, temporary, unstable and whimsical. Here today, gone like a puff of smoke tomorrow. It kind of makes you wonder if life is a dream

---

[24] Carlotta Walls LaNier, A Mighty Long Way, (New York: Ballantine Books, 1957).

or if dreams reflect life in an animated form? Could our existence on this planet be some colossal chess game being played by God and Satan, humanity being moved around at will like pawns on a chess board?

6. I have concluded therefore that man is but a mere illusion; a figment of the vivid mind of God who simply spoke us into existence, spoke us into being. God is the only reality, we are only as real as God allows us to be and then without prior notification we are erased like a mistake on paper. At His bidding, God can say live and man will live. God can say die and man will lie down and die. Paul declared on Mars Hill, "It's in Him we live and move and have our being," (Acts 17:18). Yes, Heaven and earth shall ultimately pass away.

II. Jesus said, "But my words shall not pass away."

1. It is important to note that Jesus Christ used the conjunction 'but' as if to say, though heaven and earth will pass away into oblivion (to the contrary) or (opposite of this fact) my words are perpetual. Isaiah declared, "The grass witheredth, the flower fadeth, but the word of God shall stand forever," (Isaiah 40:8).

2. Though we have never met Moses we are acquainted with him by his statement to Pharaoh Thotmas in Egypt, "Let My People Go." We never met Frederick Douglas, but we know he said, "A people without knowledge of their

past is like a tree without roots." We know Marcus Garvey through his prolific command, "Up, up you mighty race of people." We know Malcolm X for saying, "Silence can be betrayal" and we know Martin Luther King, Jr. for saying, "I've been to the mountain top and I've seen the Promised Land."

3. These individuals have long since vanished from the stage of mortality, yet their words still echo in the corridors of time. Buildings fall, governments collapse, economies crumble, yet profound words spoken in times of conflict never go away.

4. Words reflect the length, depth and the breath of humanity. Words mirror the ambition, motivation and determination of a people, be they free or enslaved, liberated or oppressed, prosperous or impoverished.

5. Have you heard someone say, "My word is my bond?" Have you heard someone say, "I'm true to my word?" People say these things because all we really have in this life is our word. All you really leave to this world is your word. The only way you can achieve enduring effectiveness on earth is through your honest, thoughtful, heartfelt words.

6. Loving, courageous words of wisdom can never die. They endure from generation to generation to generation. William Jennings Bryant proclaimed, "Truth forever on the scaffold, wrong forever on the throne, yet that scaffold sways

the future and behind that scaffold in the dim unknown stands a mighty God keeping watch over His own."[25]

III. Jesus said that His words would not pass away, because He knew that His chronological time on earth was drawing to a swift conclusion. He knew that the Jews would soon apprehend him. He knew that the many lashes, the scourging and the execution stake awaited him. From the foundations of the world, He was born to suffer and die. Death followed him in close anticipation of his imminent martyrdom. Death cloaked him like a shadow.

1. Jesus knew that His physical presence on earth would soon be no more. He knew that soon He would be carried up in a cloud, before their very eyes. Before the end engulfed Him, He wanted the world to know that He was leaving a legacy behind that could not be corrupted, decayed, destroyed or delayed by time. Listen to His words to the twelve disciples at the last supper. He said, "If ye abide in me, and my words abide in you, ye shall ask what ye will and it shall be done unto you. Herein is My Father glorified, that ye bear much fruit; So shall ye be My disciples," (John 15:7-8). His sanctified word tells us that those who hear the word and see the glory of the

---

[25] James Russell Lowell, "The Present Crisis," https://poets.org/poem/present-crisis.

word, but because of a lack of conviction, don't abide in the word, then the word does not abide in them.

2. British clergyman, John Clifford, was so impressed by the Word, he wrote, "I paused last eve beside the blacksmith's door, and heard the anvil ring, the vespers chime. And looking in I saw upon the floor old hammers, worn with beating years of time. 'How many anvils have you had?' said I, 'To wear and batter all these hammers so?' 'Just one,' he answered. Then with the twinkling eye, 'The anvil wears the hammers out, you know.' And so, I thought, the anvil of God's Word; for ages skeptics' blows have beat upon, but though the noise of falling blows was heard, the anvil is unchanged; the hammers gone."[26]

3. Jesus wanted us to know that He would not leave us empty handed, but with the word that neither Satan nor man could ever take away. His words rocked the foundations of the world. His words toppled governments. His words shook empires. His word defeated armies and sank navies.

4. John said, "In the beginning was the word, the word was with God, and the word was God. The same was in the

---

[26] John Clifford, "The Anvil of God's Word," https://www.wholesomewords.org/poetry/biblepoems/anvil.html.

beginning with God ... The word was made flesh and dwelt among us," (John1:1). The word, the alive logos, the divine utterance of God said, "He that heareth my word and believeth on Him that sent Me, hath everlasting life, and shall not pass into condemnation; but is passed from death unto life," (John5:24).

5. The word said, "The thief cometh but to kill, steal and destroy, but I am come that they might have life and have it more abundantly," (John 10:10).

6. The word said, "I am the resurrection and the life; he that believeth in Me, though He were dead, yet shall he live," (John 11:25).

**Conclusion:** The Jews accused Him, but the word would not pass away. The mob cried for His execution, but the word would not pass away. Pilate allowed Him the death penalty, but the word would not pass away. The soldiers mocked and beat Him but the word would not pass away. He shouldered our burdens and carried them up Golgotha Hill, but the word would not pass away. They nailed Him to an old rugged cross, but the word would not pass away. They murdered Him on Friday evening. Death, hell and the grave tried to constrain Him on Saturday. But the Word rose on the third day morning with all power in His hands.

His word is perpetual. His word is permanent. His word is prominent. His word is salvation. His word is redemption.

76

His word is justification. His word saved a wretch like me. His word is the power of God unto salvation. It never loses its power. It's like fire shut-up in my bones. "His word is a lamp unto my feet and a light unto my path. I'll hide His word deep in my heart that I might not sin against God," (Psalm 119:105).

**A Poet asked,** "Am I a soldier of the cross, a follower of the lamb. And shall I fear to own his cause or blush to speak His name? Must I be carried to the skies on flowery beds of ease, while others fought to win the prize and sailed through bloody seas? Sure I must fight if I would reign, increase my courage Lord! I'll bear the toil, endure the pain, supported by thy word."[27]

---

[27] Isaac Watts, "Am I a Solider of the Cross," https://www.hymnal.net/en/hymn/h/468.

# I Have Overcome the World
## John 16:33 NKJV

**Text:** These things I have spoken unto you, that in me ye might have peace. In the world ye shall have tribulation; but be of good cheer; I have overcome the world.

**Exposition:** Our text finds Jesus Christ at the tender age of 33 in A.D.29 concluding His farewell sermon to His disciples. They had journeyed together for over three years and Jesus knew that His hour of reckoning was drawing near. In this Upper Room discourse Christ speaks precious truths that both wound and heal both hurt and comfort.

1. He wounds them in that; He tells them that they shall not be welcome in and shall be put out of the same synagogues where they had worshipped all their lives. Jesus Christ wounds them even more by telling the disciples that men would try to kill them, a price bounty would be on their heads and men would think that they were doing the will of God in their execution. Were that not enough, Christ tells the disciples that He was soon to depart from them, and they could not go where He was going.

2. Then Jesus pours soothing, cool ointment on their wounds with healing words. First, He promised to send back the Holy Comforter to them. Second, Jesus Christ promised to visit them again after the resurrection. Third, Christ

promised to secure for the disciples an answer of peace to all their prayers. Fourth, Jesus Christ explained that where He was going, was back to His Heavenly Father and fifth, Jesus assured them that though they would have tribulations in this world in Him they could still find peace.

**Title: I Have Overcome the World**

**Definition:** Overcome - Conquer, subdue, defeat, over throw, surmount. In the Greek language, *Nikao* (prevail, get the victory).

I. In our lives Satan and the forces of evil are trying every way imaginable to overcome God's children.

1. The evil one employs everything from A to Z that he may overcome you. He will use animosity, backstabbing, criticism, debts, envy, fraud, greed, hate, ignorance, jealousy, killing, lust, malice, narcotics, oppression, poverty, quarreling, racism, sin, terrorism, unbelief, viciousness, war. He would have us yielding to temptation, x-raying other people's business, while acting zany as a clown.

2. Satan has always desired to rule mankind. He has always wanted to show God that if given a chance, He could overcome us with His lies and temptations. After going to and fro, up and down the earth, seeking whom He could devour, the devil asked God to remove the hedge from around Job so that He could vex Job until He cursed

God to His face. Though He took all that Job had and even made him sick, Job said, "All the days of my appointed time I will wait on the Lord until my change come. He is determined to bring you down. Peter, the senior apostle was so high on Satan's hit list that at the last supper celebration Jesus Christ told the former fisherman, "Simon, Simon, behold Satan hath desired to have you, that he may sift you as wheat ... He wants to dissect you, expose you, break you down and shake you up until you crumble to nothing.

3. Satan is mad this morning. He's mad that you are in the pavilion of the Lord. He is mad that many of you are saved. He is mad that many of you are not ashamed of the gospel of Jesus Christ. Because Satan is so furious with you, Jesus Christ promised," Ye shall have trials and tribulations". The world will hate you. Men will persecute you. Friends will despise you. Family will turn and walk away from you. Society will segregate you. People on your job will constantly test you. Those who are not in Christ will call you a holy roller, a goody goody, a Jesus freak. But take heart, have faith, only trust Him, for Jesus Christ said in Revelation 3:21, "To Him that overcometh will I grant to sit with me in my throne, even as I also overcame, and am set down with My Father in His throne."

4. A poet asked, "Must I be carried to the skies on flowery beds of ease, while others fought to win the prize, and sailed thru bloody seas?  Sure, I must fight if I would reign; I crease my courage. Lord! I'll bear the toil, endure the pain, supported by thy, Word."[28]

II. Though Satan will throw various stumbling blocks in our paths, all His contemptible efforts, all his evil labors are nullified by the matchless peace that we are able to secure in Jesus Christ our Lord.

1. It is the will of Jesus Christ that regardless of external factors, no matter what is going on outside, there is still unexplainable Shalom, peace within the hearts of His beloved. Ezekiel said, "It is as it were a wheel in the middle of a wheel," (Ezekiel 1:16). When the world outside is cruel and cold Jeremiah said, "His word was in my heart as a burning fire shut up in my bones," (Jeremiah 20:9).

2. This farewell sermon was designed to leave the disciples with a special sense of safety and security for He said, "These things have I spoken… that in me ye might have peace." Martin Luther King once declared, "True peace is not merely the absence of tension, but the presence of

---

[28]Ibid, Isaac Watts.

justice."[29] Everyone may be asleep in bed, the lights may be off, the alarm might be activated, the neighborhood quiet and though it seems peaceful, that's not true peace. That's not permanent peace.

3. Only in Christ can we find true peace. Only in Jesus can we abide in Shekinah glory. Only in the Messiah can we find supernatural, inner sanctuary peace. Micah prophesied, "This man shall be the peace," (Micah 5:5). Isaiah went a little farther and called Him "Wonderful Counselor, Mighty God, Everlasting Father, and Prince of Peace." Only through the Messiah can this old, hard, cold, mean world find peace. We need peace right now in the midst of domestic terrorist attacks and a prevailing climate of economic inequality, social unrest, moral bankruptcy and racial division.

4. In the midst of a world gone mad, we pray for peace in the Persian Gulf, Syria, Lebanon and the Sudan. We pray for peace in our homes, peace in our communities, peace in the drug infested streets, peace in our war-torn nation, peace in starving lands, peace in the White House, peace in the poor house, peace in the jailhouse, peace in the church house, peace in your life and peace

---

[29] Martin Luther King, Jr., "When Peace Becomes Obnoxious," Sermon, Dexter Avenue Baptist Church, March 18, 1956.

in my life. It was this call for precious peace that prompted Paul to tell the church of Phillipi; "And the peace of God which passeth all understanding, shall keep your hearts and minds through Christ Jesus," (Philippians 4:7), the giver of divine peace...

III. As Jesus concludes this powerful discourse, this moving dissertation, He reminds His disciples to be of a good cheer; for I have overcome the world.

    1. We ought to be optimistic, glad, happy, shining, and rejoicing in the knowledge that Jesus Christ has overcome the world. How can anyone who knows the Lord sit still with a mean, tight, twisted, ugly, hard cold grimace on their face, knowing that the Son of the living God has overcome this world? He triumphed, not for His own benefit, but that you and I might share in His victory, that you and I might be made heirs according to the hope of eternal life.

    2. Cheer up, hold your head up and wipe that tight, twisted, sour frown off your face. Replace it with a beautiful smile, because if you are saved, you truly have something to smile about. You may see me smile for no apparent reason; you may hear me laugh, though no one told a joke. You might hear me moan, though nothing hurts me. You might see me cry, though nobody's sad. You might see me run, though no one's

chasing me. Don't worry I'm not crazy. I'm not psychotic; I'm just intoxicated by the Holy Ghost. I'm not paranoid. I'm just glad that my Savior has made the devil a liar and overcome this world.

3. I'm glad that He healed the sick, I'm glad that He raised the dead, that He made wine out of water. I'm glad He fed the multitude with a boy's lunch. He calmed an angry sea. I'm glad that they whipped Him all night, for with His stripes I've been healed. He carried an old rugged cross up to Calvary for me. I'm glad He wore a crown of thrones on his head. I'm glad they drove spikes in His hands and feet. I'm glad the temple was rent in two and rocks split wide open. I'm glad the sun refused to shine and the graves could hold their rotting corpse no longer. He dropped his head in the locks of his shoulders. I'm glad that while I was yet a sinner Christ died for me. Yes, I'm glad; they laid Him in a grave on Friday. So glad He went through hell on Saturday and snatched the victory out of Satan's hand. Death and the grave tried to hold him down, but He rose from the dead on Sunday morning with all power in His mighty hands.

4. I can hear the Lamb of God in victory, in glory, in his majesty saying, "I have overcome the world, nothing can stop me, no chains can hold me down, Satan is defeated, I have the keys to death, hell and the grave. All power has been given unto me in heaven and earth."

**Conclusion:** I have overcome the world! You too can overcome the world, if you give your life to Jesus Christ. Keep the faith, hold on to God's unchanging hand. "In all these things, we are more than conquerors through Him that loved us," (Romans 8:37). Don't let the devil and this world steal your joy. Jesus Christ said in Revelation 2:17, "To Him that overcometh will I give to eat of the hidden manna and give Him a white stone, and in the stone a new name written, which no man knoweth saving He that receiveth it." Like Martin Luther King Jr. I too can say; "It doesn't matter with me now."[30] Hellhounds may pursue me and pain may rack my body. Sickness, death, burdens beyond measure may come, but that's all right. In Jesus Christ, in the Holy Ghost, "I've been to the mountaintop. I'm not worried about anything; I'm not fearing any man because mine eyes have seen the glory of the coming of the Lord."[31] Every now and then, when doors are shut in my face, when the valley is low and the

---

[30] Martin Luther King, Jr, "I've Been To The Mountaintop," Stanford: The Martin Luther King, Jr. Research and Education Research, 1968.
[31] Ibid.

rain falls and the way gets dark, I just lift up mine eyes unto the hills from whence cometh my help and I say:   "Ride on, King Jesus ride on. No man can hinder thee. Ride on King Jesus ride on, no man can hinder thee."[32]

---

[32] Traditional Negro Spiritual, "Ride on King Jesus," http://dailyprayer.us/Christian_song_lyrics/Christian_song_lyrics.php?s=ride_o n_king_jesus.

Part Three
Crunch Time

## Crunch Time

In the spring of 30 A.D. Jesus was a man under the pressure of public scrutiny. The poor saw Him as Savior. The rebels saw Him as a revolutionary. The merchants saw Him as a competitor. The ruling class saw Him as a nuisance. The priestly order saw Him as a superior. The apostles and disciples concluded that He was indeed the Christ, the Son of the living God.

Pressure was mounting and all eyes were focused on the God-man from Galilee, but He had His eyes focused on Jerusalem. He was deliberate in every message, every healing and even every rebuke of His opponents to reference Calvary. The horrors of crucifixion awaited Him, but He did not flee. His steps were ordered, and it was '*crunch time!*' There is a critical point in every competition when all the practice, all the rituals and all the training converge on one move, one play, one decision. *Crunch Time.* How you respond when your back is against the wall can make or break you.

In this third part, we follow Jesus to the Cross and hear Him struggle with His humanity and divinity. He speaks to us as Mary's oldest son and God's only begotten Son. The ancient kerygma is still the true core of our preaching.[33] This is what the apostles taught and preached until they paid for it with their lives. This is what we are called to do, preach Christ and Him crucified. Dead, buried and resurrected on the third day, then ascended to the right hand of God. If we fail to preach our Lord's passion, then we will not be able to preach about a God of compassion for the weak, the brokenhearted, the poor and the downtrodden. It's *crunch time* in America right now. Are we ready for the last play of the game?

If the exposition of the sermon sets the table then the introduction is somewhat of an appetizer. I often use the introduction as a teaser in presenting the total objective of the sermon. When preparing a sermon I also use the introduction as a thesis statement. Sometimes I use the introduction as a summary of what it is I want the sermon to accomplish while holding the punchline on irony of the sermon in escrow until the conclusion. It is necessary to establish a thought thread in the introduction that will run through the sermon and ultimately tie to the conclusion. The introduction is a tool that should help the preacher and the audience see the end at the beginning without the necessity of a "spoiler alert."

---

[33] Ibid, Jackson.

# Well Done
## Matthew 25:21 NKJV

**Text:** His lord said unto him, well done, thou good and faithful servant: You were faithful over a few things, I will make you ruler over many things: Enter into the joy of your lord.

**Exposition:** As Jesus Christ was approaching the climatic event of His life and heading towards the cross at Jerusalem in 29 A.D., He delivered the immortal words of the Olivet discourse. In this magnificent sermon truth and light dropped from his lips like precious pearls and radiant rubies. He spoke of signs of the end of the world as we understand and the truth that no man knowth the hour or the day when the Son of Man shall come in His glory, not even the Son, only the Father.

Jesus then enlists the aid of parables to explain the atmosphere and character of the kingdom of heaven. One of the most renown parables of Jesus is the parable of the wise and foolish servants.

**Exegesis:** Jesus said that there was a householder about to depart on a trip into a faraway land. Before he departed he assembled his servants and left each one of them with certain responsibilities. To one servant he left $5000 or five talents, (the equivalent of $1000 per talent). To one he left $2000 or two talents. To another, he left one talent or $1000. To each according to his own ability received talents.

The master went away for quite a while and when he returned he assembled the three servants to receive a report. The servant with five talents reported that he had gained five more. This pleased the householder. The servant with two also reported a 100 percent gain. Likewise, this pleased the master. But the servant with one talent made up excuses, reporting that he hid the talent or money in the ground so that he would not lose it. This angered the master and he took the slothful servants talent and gave it to the servant who already had five. Then the master cast the unprofitable servant out into utter darkness where there was weeping and gnashing of teeth.

**Introduction:** God is the heavenly house holder and we are His servants. We are given choices in life according to the grace of the Almighty. We can choose to sit on God's goodness. We can choose to be slothful with His mercy. We can choose to be lackadaisical with the ability that He has given us. Or, we can follow the paths of the obedient servants and go forth and work diligently for the Lord. We can give Him the best of our service, and when God calls us in for a report we will hear His welcome voice echo through the corridors of eternity and say…

**Title: Well Done**

I.  Life is a constant progression towards death. We are here only for a fleeting moment. Time waits for no man. If we are not careful time will pass us by.

1. Therefore, we must live each day to its fullest potential. We must make our time here on earth profitable.

2. Jesus said the harvest is plenteous, but the laborers are few. Therefore, our lives should reflect fruit reaped in love, faith, compassion and consistency.

3. In our Christian lives, we cannot take the chance of being caught with our work undone, for who can say when we will be called in to give our report.

4. We must live each day with the foresight of Job who in his time of turmoil told his friends, "I know that my redeemer liveth, and that he shall stand at the latter day upon the earth. And though after my skin worms destroy this body, yet in my flesh shall I see God," (Job 19:25).

II. Jesus teaches us in our text today that though salvation is free, yet it comes with certain responsibilities and obligations.

1. To make the parable more understandable Jesus talked about talents or money, something we all have some (if limited) contact with.

2. In a modern setting, talents can be related to the natural endowment or gifts a person has.

3. God gives all his children talents. We all have talent, or a special knack for doing certain things.

4. Your talents are not exactly like mine. My talents do not always match yours. Our talents are like finger

prints varied and different, yet we all have or have had talent.

5. A key phase in our text is the (b) clause in chapter 25:15 which tells us that the master gave talents to each servant according to his several ability.

6. This phase reveals to us that even though God gives all of us talent, He does not distribute it all evenly. He gives more to some and less to others because some people are more responsible than others. He blesses or rewards some now and others later. Someone has said, "Favor ain't fair."

7. He gives visible talent, an abundance of talent to some and invisible talent to others. Oh, how I have envied those who have musical talents to play instruments. Yet I have grown enough spiritually to realize that though I don't have the gifts of playing instruments, yet I have been endowed to preach the gospel of Jesus Christ, under the anointing of the Holy Spirit with authority and power.

8. God gives us unique talents according to our abilities for God knows us all too well. He knows what we will do and what we will not do. He knows what we mentally and physically can and cannot accomplish. That's why our elders used to say, "He will put no more on you than your soul can bear."

III. In the natural course of our lives we must take the talents that God has given us and use them wisely and consistently.

    1. If God has blessed you to teach, as he did Mary McLeod Bethune, you must use your skills of instilling knowledge to eradicate ignorance. For our people continue to perish from a lack of knowledge.

    2. If your skill is in the medical field you must labor like Dr. Charles Drew to fight disease and suffering as our Savior did with the hem of His garment.

    3. No matter what your talent may be it is a gift from God. Your talent is meant to be used for the upbuilding of God's Holy Kingdom, not to satisfy some personal agenda, get rich quick scheme or movie star ambition.

    4. When the Lord bestows great wealth of talent and ability upon you He is looking for a return on His investment. You are expected to use your God given talent to win souls for Christ, to enlighten those in the shadows of ignorance and further the cause of brotherhood among men. Remember to whom much is given, much is required.

    5. Like the good and faithful servants, it is expected of us to take five and make 10, to take two and make four to take one and make two. God expects something good from us, God expects productivity from us. God expects consistency from us. Our Christ said, "If any

man would come after me, let him deny himself, take up his cross daily and follow me," (Mark 8:34). He never said it would be easy, but He did promise to be with us always, even unto the ends of the earth.

IV. If we want to see the Lord we must shun the evil example of the servant with one talent.

1. He only received one talent because the master knew the servant was not as trustworthy, dependable, diligent and loyal as the other servants.

2. Sometimes we wonder why we don't have as much as other people have, why we are not as successful as other people are. The answer is right before our eyes. We don't dedicate ourselves to the cause like others. We don't study hard; we don't strive for the higher mark. We do not want to sweat. We do not want to get dirty. We do not want to wrinkle our clothes. We would rather stay in our own personal comfort zone and complain about what other people are doing.

3. We imitate the wicked servant. He would not step out on faith. He would not put his trust in God. He misinterpreted the assignment and figured it would be safer to hide his talent rather than lose it and be punished.

4. We still do that today! We have natural ability to do amazing things, but we would rather bury our talents

within our psychological constellations than let our light shine before men so that they may see our good work and glorify our Father which is in heaven.

5. Some of us can sing like angels, but refuse to hum a note. Some us can pray like Paul, but refuse to bend a knee. Some of us can preach like Peter, but refuse to open a bible. Some of us can teach like Aquila and Priscilla, but refuse to give instruction.

6. We waste God's talent. We sit on His blessing with our dismissive attitudes, laziness, self-righteous, and contempt. Satan binds us with fear of what others might say about us or do to us. Well my bible tells me, "If God be for us, who shall be against us," (Romans 8:31).

7. One day out of the blue, our good Master is going to return with power and great glory. His question to us shall be, what have you done with my talent? And when you answer, Master I was afraid, and I hid your talent in the earth. The good Master will take your talent and hand it over to someone who will put his talent to use.

8. Maybe that explains why so many older people cannot do the things they used to do. Could it be that they didn't do a thing with what they had when they had it? God will take your talent if you fail to use it for His

glory. Don't be fooled, there are plenty people who can do what you do better than you.

**Conclusion:** If you would let God use you all the days of your life, do your best till the end and be steadfast, unmovable, always abounding in the word of truth, you can do like Paul and finish the course, fighting the good fight of faith. Then you can imitate Job and wait on God until your change comes. Then you can join Isaiah as he walked without fainting, ran and never became weary. You will mount up on wings like an eagle, renewing your strength, restoring your joy, rekindling the flame, creating a clean heart, and energizing a right spirit within you.

If you would only trust Him and be faithful until death you will receive a crown of life. If you would do your Christian duty and stand up for Jesus, I believe that in that great getting up morning, in that great bye and bye you would hear Jehovah's welcome voice say, "Well Done, good and faithful servant." You've been through some trials. You've shed some tears. Your family has disappointed you. Loved ones have passed away. But because you kept the faith, even when your enemies pursued you. You kept the faith, though hell hounds were on your trail. Sometimes you had to stand alone. You've been lied on, cheated, talked about and mistreated. You've been rebuked and scorned. But through it all, you kept the faith! So, all I can say is, "Well Done, my good and faithful servant." You've been faithful over a few things, now I'll make you a ruler over many. Enter into the joy of the Lord.

I just want to hear Elshaddi say, "Well Done!" I want to hear Elohim say, you fought a good fight. I want to hear El Elyon say, you kept the faith, you finished the course, now come on up and claim your crown. I want to hear Adonai say, this is My son who was lost but now he is found. He was dead, but now he's forever alive.

# An Appointment in Heaven
## Luke 23:42-43 NKJV

**Text:** And he said unto Jesus, Lord, remember me when thou come into thy kingdom and Jesus said unto him, verily I say unto thee, today shalt thou be with me in paradise.

**Title: An Appointment in Heaven**

**Exposition:** Our text takes us to the place of the skull, a place called Golgotha. In the Latin tongue it is Calvary, an ancient death facility. On this hill outside Jerusalem hill we have before us three men being executed for crimes that they have committed against society. Two of them have been found guilty of grand theft, larceny. The other is charged with a more horrendous, drastic offense. He said He was the Son of God. To the Pharisees and the chief priest this was the highest form of blasphemy and so they had no other choice than to crucify him. The day is Nissan 14 or April 14, AD 30. The time is the third watch of the day or 12 noon. This is the darkest day in human history. The day when the very Christ, who came to save the children of Israel, was murdered by those to whom he was sent to redeem.

He was nailed to a rugged disfigured execution stake between two thieves. Crucified, the most ignominious death, the most shameful, demoralizing, punishment the Romans could think of. Dangling there, suspended from the earth with all heaven above watching. The focus of crucifixion was to cause

100

the victim to experience as much pain as possible. The inflicting of as much suffering as the human soul could bear: agony, starvation, insufferable thirst, suffocation and excruciating convulsions of torment were the goals of the crucifixion event.

In many cases death was slow, sometimes lingering, leaving the victim to suffer three, four, even six days. But in the case of Jesus Christ, it was all over in six hours. During this epic ordeal the bible light shines on two thieves; men of corruption, greedy, bad habits and disregard. These two were hoodlums, misfits of society, broken men, locked up on charges they could not refute. They were common crooks, thieves, malefactors, and malcontents. Punished for what they did, the two were only reaping the harvest of the bad seed they sowed. Interest paid on lives of sin.

You would imagine that at this point of no return these two outlaws would have been solemn, repentive, and prayerful. At least they should have been remorseful for the reckless, crooked paths that brought them to this dark hour.

**Exegesis:** But such was not the case here. One of the malefactors decided to join in the chorus of the hecklers and haters who challenged our Savior to save himself since he saved others. The malefactor countered their attacks with his own railing. He asked Jesus, if thou be Christ, save thyself and us? He seemed to be ambivalent to the significance of this historical moment. Here he was a sin stained man, hanging beside his and the worlds' only hope of salvation. His sarcastic plea revealed his callous nature, his lack of discipline and blatant disregard for authority. He wanted Jesus to grant him a special favor, not because he believed but because he was in a jam and the masters presence was convenient.

As he yet challenged the divinity of Jesus the other condemned man spoke up. He was more cognizant of the gravity of the moment. Somewhere he had heard about this God-man of Galilee. His life of crime had not completely robbed him of the ability to discern and comprehend. In the cold caverns of his heart the pitiful, disfigured image of this humble and meek young man ignited a flame. This man hanging in the middle was unlike him. He did not approach his execution with fear and trembling. He did not have the appearance of one who lived a life of crime, greed and folly. Even in this wounded condition he glowed like no other man could.

The condemned man knew that Jesus was innocent but close examination revealed that he was unbearably burdened with guilt and grief. The malefactor asked his belligerent comrade, "Do you not fear God, seeing that you are condemned with him? We are receiving the punishment we deserve for our crimes: but this man is innocent of any wrong." Turning to Jesus, he acknowledged the sovereignty and majesty of our Savior. He ignored the excruciating pain of the spikes in his hands and feet. He forgot the mundane long enough to grasp the eternal. He said to the master, "Lord remember me when thou comest into thy kingdom." Even on the cross Jesus continued His mission of saving the lost. The Lord, always compassionate, told him, "Verily (or truly) I say unto thee, today shalt thou be with Me in paradise." By expressing his faith in Jesus the malefactor made.

## Title: An Appointment in Heaven

I. Our text reveals to me that salvation is available to all who will receive Jesus as Savior.

1. The thief on the cross was an unlikely candidate for eternal life. His conversion on the cross confirms what Jesus said in Matthew 19:30, "But many that are first shall be last; and the last shall be first."

2. Many times we can be very judgmental as to who is or is not saved. We often attempt to predict who can or cannot be converted. Who has or has not been called.

3. We sometimes scrutinize people by how they look or how they dress or where they live in prequalifying them to receive Jesus as their personal Savior.

4. We don't want to fool with folks who fail our standards test. People who don't look like or act like or think like or believe like us are unapproachable. Just the person who needs to be witnessed to most of all is the one we avoid the most.

5. We want the world to fit into a neat little package. We want it to stay in our comfort zone. That's why that criminal on the cross waited until he was at the brink of death to reach out to Jesus.

6. All of his life he had been rejected of men. Born poor on the wrong side of the tracks, he had to make it with the bare minimum. He was dirty, unkept, untrained, unmanageable. The only way he knew to survive was to take what he needed. He could not enter the temple or synagogue he was unclean. He did not come from the right family. He lacked the educational background. He did not have any church clothes.

7. He was part of the so called bad element. You know, those whom we have labeled undesirable. Like the alcoholic, the dope addict, the physically and mentally impaired, the prostitute, street walkers, prison bound, uncouth, unsophisticated, poverty stricken, homeless and disenfranchised, he too was always on the outside looking in.

8. He had been pushed aside and excluded for so long that eventually he simply acquiesced to society's stigmas. He wore their label of misfit. He was the stereotypical outcast.

II. While this common thief was forgotten by men, yet he is still precious in the sight of God. He somehow fit into God's plan for humanity.

1. Man loves because of one's character, appearance, affiliation, education, association, fame, fortune or physique.

2. God loves not because of, but in spite of. He looks beyond faults and recognizes our needs. He loves us with agape. He loves unconditionally. He loves us with our several flaws and short comings. His love knows no limits no bottom or top. No mountain high or valley low. That's why Paul could boast, "Nothing can separate us from the love of God, which is in Christ Jesus our Lord," (Romans 8:33). John wrote, "Behold what manner of love the Father hath bestowed upon us, that we should be called the sons of God," (1 John 3:1).

3. The bad man whom society shunned and cast aside was still God's creation. The good Lord had watched over him all of his life. Even when he had done wrong and been in bad places, committing unconscionable atrocities against society, God cared for him. At his lowest low, he was still God's property. Even in the low down gutters of human insurrection he could not escape the projectile of God's grace and mercy. The far reaching hand of God can locate even the most remote fugitive.

4. I'm so glad that unlike man, God never gives up on any of us. We lock people away and forget about them, call them useless, good for nothing, a waste. God can take that same man or woman we condemned and use them for His glory. That's why He sent the prophet to the potter's house in Jeremiah 18, so that he could observe that our God, upon finding a flaw in man, can tear man

down and make, mold and reshape man as he sees fit. For it is in Him we live, move and have our being (Acts 17:28).

5. While we prejudge and condemn people based on our knowledge and our experiences, God is using that same individual for greatness. Ask Paul, formerly known as Saul, a bounty hunter for Christians. He will tell you, "What the enemy meant for evil, God meant it for good to save much people alive," (Genesis 50:20).

6. Some of you might have suffered some setbacks in your life. You might have been deprived of pleasure and position. Maybe you were laughed at in school or ridiculed or overlooked by your peers. Some of you might have come from broken homes with more tears than laughter. Maybe you are from the wrong side of the tracks or the rough side of the mountain.

7. No matter where you've been or what you're going through, one thing is for certain, you didn't make it on your own. You didn't do it by yourself. There are no self-made people. When someone tells you, 'I'm a self-made man,' know beyond a shadow of a doubt that they are lying. God has watched over and kept us all the days of our lives. It is He who has made us and not we ourselves. God has a plan for your life. I know God will use you in spite of you.

III. In the parable of the laborers in the vineyard in Matthew 20 the bible says that a landowner went into the marketplace to find willing workers for harvesting his crops. He hired each man at a penny a day. The first group of men he hired at 6 a.m. The next group at 9 a.m. The next group at 12 noon. Another group at 3 p.m. and a final group at 5 p.m. When it was time to pay the workers at the end of the day they all received a penny. Those hired at the beginning were upset because those hired at the end of the day received the same pay as they did. The landowner told them to take their pay and go. They agreed on a wage and he paid them the agreed upon amount. It was his money and he could pay the last hired the same as the first hired if he so desired. Such is the kingdom of heaven.

1. That encourages me because I know that God does not play favorites. He does not care about who we think we are. There are three prisms of man. 1) How other people see us, 2) How we see ourselves and, 3) How God really sees us. The first two are distortions; the final one is crystal clear.

2. God does not care about our bios or resumes. He is not impressed by our plaques or trophies. He never considers our diplomas, degrees or certificates. Meritorious service, memberships or Medals of Honor don't impress God. Longevity and repetition doesn't move God. Long standing tradition and custom means

diddle to a God who once said, "Let there be light, and there was light." What could we ever do to move the immutable, un-moveable God?

3. Your being saved way back when does not make you anymore saved then someone new, right here, right now! Don't be fooled by superstition and heresy. Once saved always saved. Our God is able to do it right the first time. Salvation is not based on merit, manipulation or money. It has no tiers or levels or grades or stages or pyramid schemes. *Soteria,* salvation is free, for His grace is sufficient to supply every need.

4. Maybe that's why the poet wrote, "If religion was a thing that money could buy, the rich would live and the poor would die."[34]

5. Our salvation is based on our faith in our Lord and Savior, Jesus the Christ who said, "Only believe." He told the woman, "Thy faith hath saved thee." Paul told us, "If thou shall confess with thy mouth the Lord Jesus and believe in thine heart that God hath raised him from the dead thou shalt be saved. For with the heart man believeth unto righteousness: and with the mouth confession is made unto salvation," (Romans 10:9-10).

---

[34] Pete Seeger, "All My Trials," American Favorite Ballads, Vol. 4, 1961.

**Conclusion:** You should be glad that no matter where you've been, no matter how wretched you are, no matter how many times you've been rejected by the world, you can still make an appointment in heaven.

Job declared, "For I know that my redeemer lives and that He shall stand at the latter day up on the earth. And though after my skin worms destroy this body, yet in my flesh, shall I see God; Whom shall I see for myself, and mine eyes shall behold, and not another," (Job 19:25-27).

No matter how much you are criticized by men, God still retains the last word on your soul. No matter how many times the adversary says no, Jesus is waiting to say yes! If you are lost in your sins, Jesus is ready to find you.

You might think your sins are too filthy, beyond repair but the Lord says, "Come let us reason together, though your sins be as scarlet, they shall be white as snow; though they be red like crimson they shall be as wool," (Isaiah 1:18). He wants to save you not later, but right now! I'm glad today that from the gutter most, even to the uttermost, Jesus saves. On skid row and on death row, Jesus still saves. From the poor house to the White House, Jesus saves. From the cradle to the death bed, Jesus saves. From life's crossroads to the man on the cross, Jesus saves. If you accept him today, he will make an appointment for you in heaven.

For it is appointed unto men, once to die and then the judgment. Jesus Christ said, "In My Father's house are many mansions. I go to prepare a place for you, that where I am ye may be also," (John 14:3). The songwriter, William Couper proclaimed, "There is a fountain filled with blood drawn from Immanuel's veins, and sinners plunged beneath that flood lose all their guilty stains. The dying thief rejoiced to see that fountain in his day, and there may I, though vile as he washes all my sins away."

# Will God Ever Forsake Us?
## Matthew 27:46 NKJV

**Text:** And about the ninth hour Jesus cried with a loud, voice, saying Eli, Eli, Lama sabach thani? That is to say, my God, my God why hast thou forsaken me?

**Exposition:** The crucifixion of Jesus reveals to us a strange paradox of human and divine nature. Five days prior to his murder Christ was being heralded by a great multitude with acclamations of Hosanna, Son of David on Palm Sunday or Nissan, April 9, 30 A.D. Before a week could pass that same crowd would sing with one voice, "Crucify Him," on Nissan 14, 30 A.D. It seems so unfair that Jesus, who had out smarted the wise, Jesus who had exposed the vain arrogance of the powerful, Jesus who healed the sick, raised the dead, opened blind eyes, unclogged deaf ears and fed hungry multitudes, would die at the hands of the very people he was sent to *soter* (save, redeem or reconcile from hell).

God had spared Jesus Christ from birth. From Satan's vain temptation in the wilderness, through the different traps laid by the Pharisees and Scribes, He slipped through all their traps but this one. Only 33 years old, still young, still vibrant, still strong and healthy. He still had so much to do, so many lives to change, so many miracles to perform, so many hearts to heal and so many souls to save. Why God, why the cross? Why this shameful, agonizing, ignominious, excruciating form of capital punishment?

Then, about the ninth hour or 3 p.m. Christ could hold out no longer. He asked His Father a poignant question from his mortal soul, "My God, My God, why hast thou forsaken me?"

**Title: Will God Ever Forsake Us?**

**Definition:** Key word forsake (*Greek: en-kat-al-I-po*) to desert, quit, give up, abandon. In essence, it is to leave someone high and dry.

I.   To put this question in the proper perceptive, we must understand the context in which it was said...

    1.   When Jesus Christ said in Luke 21:9, "When ye shall hear of wars and commotion, be not terrified? For these things must first come to pass; but the end is not by and by," he spoke as a prophet.

    2.   When Jesus Christ said in Luke 19:10, "I am come to seek and save that which was lost," He spoke as the Messiah.

    3.   When Jesus Christ said in Mark 4:39, "Peace be still!" He spoke as El Shaddi, Almighty God, Adonai, and Lord of Lords.

    4.   But His question upon Calvary's cross was personalized. His question in desperation and suffering, was not that of a prophet, nor Messiah nor God, but that of a human being. His cry was that of a man, a frail and fragile living

creature, Mary's oldest son. "My God, My God, why have you forsaken me?"

II.  In our human existence we may sometime wonder; Has God forsaken me?

1.  Pastors often ask God in the midst of church turmoil and crisis, "Lord why have you abandoned me? Lord why have you turned away from me?"

2.  There are times when nothing seems to go the way they should go in our opinion. We question our faith. We even challenge God's faithfulness.

3.  Our well laid plans fall apart and we begin to question our mental capacity.

4.  High expectations create deep let downs. We never factor in the setbacks and heart breaks when we are at the drawing board.

5.  Unemployment rises in the face of financial instability and economic inequity, causing distrust in institutions originally designed to rescue the perishing.

6.  Debts seem to pile high when money is lowest and needs are severe.

7.  Scandals run rampant fueling rumors and suggestions that question ones character and original motivation.

8.  Family crisis pop up and make us wonder if all the hard work was only a front to cover up a cycle of emptiness, pain and generation dysfunction.

III.  Trials, tribulations, woes and worries, sickness and death at the most unexpected times, make us question our very existence on this earth.

1.  These troubles make us ask the Almighty, "What did I do to deserve, this grief? Why God? Why me? What about my faithfulness, does that not count to my credit? God why have you turned your back on me? Why hast thou forsaken me? Why did you let mother, father, sister or brother die? My heart is broken. My head is hung. My spirit is vexed.

2.  In a time of trouble we must not doubt the prudence and the holy providence of Jehovah God.

3.  There is a divine purpose in all that the Lord does. His every move is just. His every thought is perfect. His every utterance is holy. His center is everywhere. His circumference is unsearchable.

4.  There will be times in our life that the way seems dark, the mountains are high and the valleys are low. Though the day seems hot and the night seems endless, I know for myself, that the Lord will never forsake us. God will never leave your soul in shame.

5.  The Lord Jesus said, "In this world ye shall have tribulation but be of good cheer, for I have overcome the world," (John 16:33).

6. David said, "I have never seen the righteous forsaken nor his seed begging bread," (Psalms 37:25).

7. Job declared, "Thou He slay me yet will I trust Him...," (Job 13:15).

**Conclusion:** Though the Lord did not spare His only begotten Son on Golgotha Hill that Friday afternoon so long ago there is a happy ending. Early on the succeeding Sunday, Jesus defeated death, hell and the grave. God raised Jesus Christ up from the dead in splendor, majesty, power and glory. Hallelujah!

Will God ever forsake us? No, He will never leave your side. Continue to cry out to Him. He may not get there when you want Him, but He's always right on time. So when your enemies pursue you and the hellhounds get on your trail remember, God will never forsake you. Jesus declared in His farewell message, "Lo I am with you always even unto the ends of the earth," (Matthew 28:20).

At some point sickness will invade your home. Death will violate your family circle. But God will never forsake you. Elshaddi is a strong deliverer. Yes, God is a keeper. David triumphantly declared," In a time of trouble He shall hide me in His pavilion. In the secret of His tabernacle shall He hide me. He shall set me upon a rock," (Psalm 27:5).

Ludie Pickett summed it up in a hymn:" I've seen the lightening flashing. And heard the thunder roll, I've felt sin's breakers dashing which tried to conquer my soul; I've heard the voice of my Savior, He bid me still fight on. He promised never to leave me. Never to leave me alone."[35]

---

[35] Ludie Carrington Day Pickett, "I've Seen the Lightening Flashes," https://www.hymnal.net/en/hymn/h/688.

## It is Finished

## John 19:30 KJV

**Text:** When Jesus had received the vinegar, he said, "It is finished"; and he bowed his head and gave up his spirit.

**Title: It is Finished**

**Exposition:** Our text thrusts us upon a hill overlooking Jerusalem. An incredible series of supernatural events has taken place in the last three hours. Since high noon, a solar eclipse has engulfed the planet and darkness has permeated the light. Atmospheric pressure from the host of heaven looking down upon Jerusalem has mysteriously caused large stone formations to explode or tear in twain. The earth being altered from its natural rotation, begins to quake, shaking dead saints from rotting graves. Were these events not traumatic enough, the veil of the temple which separated the most holy place from the holy place was mysteriously ripped from top to bottom. Thus, the barrier separating mankind from the very presence of God is no more.

Now as the third watch of the day draws to a close, this man between men senses that the end is near. His final breaths are exacerbated. A Roman soldier offers Him a drink of bitter wine to relieve His rabid thirst. He takes a sip and declares in triumph, "It is Finished!"

**Introduction:** What a peculiar declaration coming from a man who had been so publicly defrocked. The statement alone is uncommon from a dying man and the victorious tenor in which Jesus reveled in the thought, makes us adore Him that much more. It is finished. Though His life's work had concluded with the shame, horror and agony of an execution stake, yet He felt victorious enough to hold His head up and say with His final breath, *"Autos esti teleo."* It is finished.

I.  If I could book a seat on a great aircraft offering its passengers the opportunity to travel back in time, I would inquire of the conductor as to whether the ship could stop at the cross of Calvary on April 14th A.D. 30 at 3:00 pm. Approaching the Master, I would dare to interrupt His final breath with a question. Out of sheer curiosity and partial ignorance, I would inquire, Lord Jesus, what is this 'It' that you have declared, "Is finished?"

1. I believe that the Lamb of God would reply, "Young man, it refers to the fact that I have executed the great designs of the Almighty."

2. In me, God saw the light that 'It' was good.

3. In me, there was a firmament in the midst of the waters and 'It' divided the waters from the waters.

4. In me, God planted the grass and herbs and flowers and trees and all types of vegetation and saw that 'It' was good.

118

5. When my Father designed man in our own image and gave him dominion over all the earth, I was the One who made sure that when God reviewed His handiwork, 'It' was good.

6. Thirty years from now, a fellow named Paul will write a letter to the church at Colossae from a Roman prison and declare that by Me were all things created that are in heaven and in earth, visible and invisible, whether they be thrones, or dominions, or principalities, or powers: all things were created by Me and for Me (Colossians 1:16).

7. Now to complete Jehovah's divine demand for justice, I have personally become sin. Though sin is repulsive to My nature, I have taken sin upon Myself. My beloved friend John will declare, "He is the propitiation for our sins, and not for ours only, but also for the sins of the whole world." One of my accusers, even the high priest Caiaphas has said, "It is expedient for us that one Man should die for the people and that the whole nation perish not."

8. Nineteen centuries from now, a songwriter will proclaim that I paid it all and that he owes me all. Sin had left a crimson stain, but I washed 'It' white as snow.

It is finished, is indicative of the fact that...

II.     I have satisfied the great demands of His justice and the mighty stream of His righteousness.

    1.   When the Lord sent rains upon the earth 40 days and nights, as the waters increased, I am the 'It' that lifted the ark above the earth.

    2.   In theophany, I was sent on a fact-finding mission. With my report complete, 'It' came to pass that Sodom and Gomorrah were destroyed by God.

    3.   I satisfied His justice when I caused Pharaoh's defeat at the opening and closing of the Red Sea; and 'It' came to pass.

    4.   'It' was I who appeared before Joshua with my sword drawn and told the warrior to loose his shoes, for the place where he was standing was holy ground. And 'It' came to pass seven days later that the walls of Jericho came tumbling down.

    5.   'It' was I who appeared to Gideon in the midst of Israel's oppression. I so confused the armies of the Midianites, that they rose against one another and Gideon destroyed them with 300 trumpet blowing, pitcher breaking soldiers of Israel.

It is finished means...

III.    I have accomplished all that was written in the prophets, and suffered the utmost malice of my enemies:

1. In Genesis, I bruised the serpent's head.

2. In Numbers, I am the star of Jacob and the Scepter that shall rise out of Israel to smite the corners of Moab and destroy all the children of Seth.

3. I was born where Micah said I would be in Bethlehem of Judea.

4. Innocent children died in Herod's search to destroy me as Jeremiah proclaimed.

5. Hosea foretold that my parents would flee to Egypt to hide me among the brown people.

6. The Psalmist knew that I would run the moneychangers out of the temple.

7. *Zechariah* saw me riding into Jerusalem on a donkey's colt and said, "Shout, oh daughter of Israel."

8. Isaiah saw me as a great light, shining among the people that walked in darkness. He further commended me, calling attention to My being born of a virgin and carrying the government on my shoulders. He called my name Wonderful, Counselor, Mighty God, Everlasting Father and Prince of Peace.

IV.  Yet, in all this glory, the prophet declared that I would be despised and rejected of men; a Man of sorrow, acquainted with grief. He said, "I am as a Lamb to the slaughter and as a sheep dumb before Her shearers," (Isaiah 53:7).

1. Daniel said, "I would be cut off, but not for myself," (Daniel 9:26).
2. David declared that I would be betrayed by one of my, so-called, friends.
3. Zechariah even knew how much the bounty for My life would be; 30 pieces of silver, enough to purchase a final resting place for the treasurer, Judas Iscariot.
4. The Psalmist previewed the lies and heard the ring of the hammer as they nailed Me to this cross. He saw them mocking Me as I hang here between two criminals, while Roman soldiers roll dice for my clothes.

**Conclusion:** But 'It' is all right now. I've been to the mountaintops. I've seen the Promised Land. I've been in the valley and I've prayed in Gethsemane. In my sufferings, the way to the holy of holies is made manifest for all who believe, through my blood.

I interrupted Him briefly to ask, "What do you mean, Jesus?" He replied, "Through my bloodshed, you now have a high priest in the order of Melchizedek, an eternal priest who never dies, but reigns forever." Such a high priest who became like unto sin. Yet, this priest has no need to make sacrifice first for His sin and then the sins of others." For today, I make one sacrifice for all, forever and then I sit down at the right hand of God in glory.

I know 'It' was an awful, excessive, extravagant price to pay, but 'It' was worth every drop of My innocent blood. For you see Son, without the shedding of blood, there is no remission of sin. That's why I said, It is finished! I've done what I came to do. It is finished! I've made right Adam's wrong. It is finished! I've unlocked prison doors. It is finished! I've allowed lost men and women, a chance at eternal life. It is finished! I've paid the ransom for mankind's redemption. It is finished! They thought they were hurting me by nailing me to this cross, but they were really helping me fulfill my prophecy. I told them that I, if I be lifted up from the earth, I'll draw all men unto me. I can give up the ghost now. It is finished! Into His hands I commend my spirit. I've fought the good fight. I've kept the faith. I've finished my course. It is finished!

My heart was broken because my Savior was about to die. Tears flowed down my cheeks. But just as I was about to break down and lament, I heard the voice of Jesus say, "Wait a minute son. Stop your weeping. I said, "It is finished but I never said I'm finished." Sure, I'm going to die. I'm going to be laid in your grave. Your name should be on the tomb. But don't panic, while you were yet a sinner, I died for you. I'll sleep Friday night and go down into hell and shake the devil until he relinquishes the keys of death, hell and the grave on Saturday. But early on Sunday morning, victory is mine. I'll walk through the grave and make a mockery of death. I'll rise again, with all power in my hands. I'll meet my disciples in Galilee and before their eyes ascend to the right hand of my Father. I'll send back a comforter for you on the day of Pentecost. I'll give John a revelation of the New Jerusalem from the Isle of Patmos.

It is finished! Satan is a defeated foe. It is finished! Death has lost its sting. Grave has no victory. It is finished! Jesus is the Author and Finisher of our faith; who for the joy that was set before Him, endured the cross, despising the shame, and is set down on the right hand of the throne of God (Hebrews 12:2). He is the Alpha and Omega; the beginning and the end; the first and the last. The faithful witness of all that was, all that is and all that ever shall be (Revelation 22:13). *It is finished!*

Part Four
Passing the Baton

## Passing the Baton Introduction

There comes a time in every life that the reality of expiration is unavoidable. This discomfort is heightened by the mystery of where, when, and above all, how. We want to know but don't really want to know, "How will I die?"

That was not the case with Jesus of Nazareth. His life was a continuous march towards Calvary. He was marked for death from the start. Even as an infant, the government tried to exterminate Him, causing His family to take asylum in Africa. As He launched His ministry, attempts were made to stone Him to death and even capsize the boat He sailed on and drown Him in the Galilee. Death followed Him in close proximity, but He never allowed the shadows to deter Him from the ultimate goal; "Upon this rock I will build My church and the gates of hell shall not prevail against it," (Matthew 16:20).

Our Lord knew all the details of His demise before the foundations of the world and so He tutored and trained His apostles and disciples to; "Go ye into all the world, baptizing them in the name of the Father and the Son and the Holy Ghost, teaching them to observe all things whatsoever I have commanded you and lo, I am with you always even unto the end of the world," (Matthew 28:18-20).

In this fourth chapter we view the post-resurrection church in its infancy. The authors are speaking to 21ˢᵗ century issues through ancient lenses. They challenged the first century status quo with revolutionary paradigms about a common carpenter who was also the manifestation of the living God. They preached about principals that were difficult to defend in such a harsh and brutal era of history; love, forgiveness, reconciliation, humility and kindness. They shook up the world because they carried a message of hope to marathon runners. Jesus passed the baton of the gospel to a most unlikely group of sprinters and gave them no choice but to, *go!* Our only hope to save this wounded world is to grab that baton and do likewise.

In this fourth and final section the conclusion demands our attention. Everything we do in sermon preparation is to finally arrive at a powerful conclusion. All the points, critical analysis, life application, relevant questions and transitions point to the conclusion of the sermon. The conclusion is the final proposition which is arrived at after the consideration of all evidence, arguments or premises. For sermon purposes the conclusion normally solidifies and summarizes the complete thought of the manuscript.[36] I often develop the conclusion at the beginning of writing the sermon and build the document with the end in view. Your audience will recall different aspects of your sermon, but the conclusion will usually have the most impact.

---

[36] Ibid, Jackson.

# What Goes Up, Must Come Down
## Acts 1:9-11 RSV

**Text:** And when he had said this, as they were looking on, he was lifted up, and a cloud took him out of their sight. And while they were gazing into heaven as he went, behold, two men stood by them in white robes, and said, "Men of Galilee, why do you stand looking into heaven? This Jesus, who was taken up from you into heaven, will come in the same way as you saw him go into heaven."

**Title: What Goes Up, Must Come Down**

**Exposition:** Acts of the Apostles is the history book of the New Testament. It looks at the defining events of the formation of the early church, through the eyes of one of the bibles greatest historians, the physician Luke, travel companion of Paul.

Acts of the Apostles is the book that links the gospels to the epistles or letters. In the gospels Jesus instructs the disciples and issues to them the great commission to 'Go'. In Acts, our Savior's instructions are manifest in the ministries of his disciples and his mission mandate is implemented through the work of His evangelist.

The last recorded events of Matthew, Mark, Luke, and John are interwoven into the fabric of Acts and even summarized in Acts 1:8, "But ye shall receive power, after that the Holy Ghost is come upon you: and ye shall be witness unto me both in Jerusalem and in all Judea and in Samaria and unto the uttermost part of the earth."

Luke is meticulous in offering details of miracles and messages, yet Acts of the Apostles, penned around 68 A.D. is an incomplete book, because it announces the Holy Spirit or post-resurrection era. We are living in the pre-eschatological or pre-apocalyptic era today. Therefore, this great journal is incomplete, still under construction and still developing even as we speak.

**Introduction:** Our text takes us to the Mount of Olives, a hill overlooking the region called Galilee. Forty days earlier, the Messiah hung on the cross between heaven above and earth below. Forty days earlier, he dropped his head and died while hanging on the cross with His Father in heaven above looking down, His beloved mother on earth beneath his feet looking up. Now the risen Savior assembled His beloved together to bid them farewell. During the last 40 days He prepared them by showing Himself alive, walking with them, breaking bread with them, allowing them to examine Him. Jesus did this to dispel any untruth spread by the Jews and reinforce the foundation He had carefully laid for the *ekklesia* or the church of the living God. His task complete, His final commandment to them was to go to Jerusalem and wait on the promised *pneuma* or *paraclete, ruach hakodesh* or Holy Spirit, literally meaning; one called alongside, advocate, counselor and comforter.

**Exegesis:** When Jesus had concluded these and other sayings, even as they looked upon Him, God called His only begotten Son back home to heaven. His mission was accomplished. He defeated death, hell and the grave. He paid the ransom note for our many sins with His precious life. Now, cloaked in the garment of humanity, He was ready to return with a glorified body, to heavenly divinity. The Bible says that He was taken up! Before their very eyes He ascended from the earth into a cloud where He was engulfed in Shekinah glory and disappeared from their sight.

Can you even imagine the awesomeness of this great miracle? Can you fathom the life-changing impression this must have made upon the disciples? Can you even identify the well spring of emotions that must have exploded in the caverns of their minds? On the one hand they despaired over their master's departure. On the other hand they rejoiced in that Jesus was going to prepare a place for them, that where He is, we may be also. No wonder they looked (*atenizo*) or gazed intently or steadfastly toward heaven. They could not believe their eyes. He just up and left them standing there.

But he did not leave them hopeless for while the disciples were yet looking up to heaven, Jesus dispatched two angels to deliver another great promise. The angels said, "Why are you men of Galilee standing around looking up into heaven? This same Jesus which is taken up from you into heaven, shall surely come back one day in the same manner." In other words, don't worry;

**Title: What Goes Up, Must Come Down**

**Definition:** One of the elementary truths of physics is Sir Isaac Newton's law of gravity which simply states, "The force of attraction between any two masses in the universe is directly proportional to the product of the masses and inversely proportional to the square of the distance between their centers of mass."[37]

For our use today this simply says to us, "Mass (in this instance Jesus the Christ) drawn from mass (in this instance the earth) to another point in the universe (that being heaven) will at some point be drawn back to the dimensional center (that being the earth) from which it came. For all practical purposes this essentially means $E=MC^2$ or;

**Title: What Goes Up, Must Come Down**

I. The ascension of Jesus is one of the basic or core beliefs of the church. His ascension into heaven enhanced his declaration of John 12:32, "And I, if I be lifted up from the earth will draw all men unto me."

-----

[37] Isaac Newton, "Newton's Law of Universal Gravitation," *Lumen Learning,* https://courses.lumenlearning.com/boundless-physics/chapter/newtons-law-of-universal-gravitation/.

1. Ascension was not exclusive to Jesus the Christ. The Bible tells us in Genesis 5:24, "Enoch walked with God and was not; for God took him."

2. Ascension happened to Elijah in 1 King 2:11, "And it came to pass, as they still went on and talked that behold: there appeared a chariot of fire, and horse of fire, and parted them both a sunder; and Elijah went up by a whirlwind into heaven."

3. Jewish literature outside the canon of the Bible developed long stories and explanations of ascensions of many religious heroes including Moses, yet these are unsubstantiated.

4. But the ascension of Jesus is on a higher level. Whereas Enoch and Elijah ascended into heaven having never known death, our Savior indeed died upon the cross, was laid in a grave and rose upon the third day morning. In that He physically died and physically rose from the dead, His ascension is a complete victory over the forces of Satan and the world. Indeed, our Savior said, "Be of a good cheer for I have overcome the world," (John 16:33).

5. We claim a personal victory in our Savior's ascension which signals to us the splendid rapture of the glorified Son, with the Omnipotent Father. When we first saw Jesus, it was as the King of the Jews, the offspring of David, the root of Jesse. Now in full dominion, He wears a greater crown, King of all that is, all that was, and all

that ever will be. For He told His disciples, "All power is given unto Me in heaven and in earth," (Matthew 28:18).

6. His crucifixion and resurrection were geographically limited to Palestine. Yet, His holy ascension embraces an unlimited universal heavenly dimension.

7. Enoch and Elijah were friends of God, but this Jesus is God's only begotten Son. Enoch and Elijah, though they were close to God, they did not know how God was going to elevate them. Their ascension was a surprise.

8. But Jesus knew that He would ascend. He said in John 6:26, "What and if ye shall see the Son of Man ascend up where He was before?" Likewise, He told Mary Magdalene, "Touch Me not; for I am not yet ascended to My Father: but go to My brethren, and say unto them, I ascend unto My Father and your Father; and to My God, and your God," (John 20:17).

9. Jesus already knew that which came to pass, for He told His disciples at the last supper; I came forth from the Father, and am come into the world: again, I leave the world, and go to the Father (John 16:28).

II. We have a blessed inheritance in our Savior's ascension. For now He reoccupies a Holy seat that only the Son of God could fulfill. For only Jesus could sit down on the right hand of God in glory. For there is supreme power in God's right hand.

1. David knew that there is salvation on Jehovah's right hand. He declared, "Now know I that the Lord saveth His anointed; He will hear Him from His holy heaven with the saving strength of His right hand," (Psalm 20:6).

2. I'm so happy that I have somebody who cares so much for me. I'm glad that I have someone who looks beyond my faults and identifies my needs. I've got somebody who will take up for me. I've got somebody who will face my enemies in the heat of battle. I've got somebody who will stand in the gap (a middle man) interceding on my behalf. "The Lord said unto my Lord, sit thou at my right hand, until I make thine enemies thy footstool," (Psalm 110:1).

3. Jesus had to ascend to the right hand of God, in order that He might secure my new home. Jesus said, "In my Father's house are many mansions: if it were not so, I would have told you. I go to prepare a place for you," (John 14:2). I'm so glad He's up there building my room right now!

4. It makes me happy, when I recall how they took Him to trial and yet He never said a mumbling word. But when they asked Him if He was the Christ, Jesus said, "I am and ye shall see the Son of Man sitting on the right hand of power and coming in the clouds of heaven," (Mark 14:62).

5. I'm esthetic that He did not hang around. I'm glad, that He didn't beat around the bush. He did not hesitate, nor did He vacillate. Mark wrote, "So then after the Lord had spoken unto them, He was received up into heaven, and sat on the right hand of God," (Mark 16:19).

6. I'm looking forward to seeing him when I surrender my labors and pick up my reward. Stephen said, "Behold, I see the heavens opened, and the Son of man standing on the right hand of God," (Acts 7:56).

7. I have no need to go to the priest for confession. I don't have to make a pilgrimage to Mecca. I don't have to consult the wisdom of Confucius. Nor, do I need to become enlightened through meditations with a Buddhist monk.

8. I have a high priest. One in the Holy, royal order of Melchizedek, priest king of Salem, king of peace. My high priest "made one sacrifice for all man's sins forever, and then he sat down on the right hand of God," (Hebrew 10:12).

III. Wait a minute .You told us, what goes up must come down. You said $E=MC^2$, and yet all you've told us about is Jesus going up and sitting at the right hand of God. What comes down?

1. Well birds go up, but when their wings become tired, they come down to earth to rest. Airplanes go up, but when

they run low on fuel, they must come down. Space shuttles blast off, but after they orbit the earth so many times they too must come down.

2. Elevators go up, but upon the command of a pushed button, they come down. The stock market goes up, but a change in the interest rate will quickly bring it down.

3. The sun comes up in the east and goes down on the western slopes. Hem lines go up on skirts, but as soon as the style changes, they come down again. Gas prices go up, but when supply exceeds demand it comes down. Crack heads get high only to crash and burn.

4. Even Jesus went up on the cross and came down to a borrowed tomb. **Transition:** When saints rejoice and get on one accord; when God's children shout for joy; when the elect wave Holy hands; when Christians let go and let God, then we experience what I call the law of spiritual gravity or $B=PW^2$ ... In other words, when praises go up, blessings will come down!

**Conclusion:** Church get ready! For herein lies our blessed hope. "This same Jesus which is taken up from you into heaven, shall so come in like manner as ye have seen Him go into heaven," (Acts 1:11b). I'm looking for that great *Parousia,* the second coming of my Lord ...

I have no idea when He's coming. I don't know to where He's coming. I was not asked to serve on the time and place committee. But, when I accepted Him as my personal Savior, I volunteered for the welcome committee. I'm waiting for the holy apocalypse. Paul said, "And to you who are troubled rest with us, when the Lord Jesus shall be revealed from heaven with His mighty angels," (2 Thessalonians 1:7). I'm praying for *epiphaneia*. "I charge thee therefore before God, and the Lord Jesus Christ, who shall judge the quick and the dead at His appearing and His kingdom," (2 Timothy 4:1).

How will we recognize Him when He returns? "Beloved, now are we the sons of God, and it doth not yet appear what we shall be: but we know that, when He shall appear, we shall be like Him; for we shall see Him as He is," (1 John 3:2). Pastor what about this old worn out body of mine? Don't worry! "For our conversation is in heaven; from whence also we look for the Savior, the Lord Jesus Christ: Who shall change our vile body, that it may be fashioned like unto His glorious body, according to the working whereby He is able even to subdue all things unto Himself," (Philippians 3:21). Be ready, when He cracks the skies like glass and parts the air. No matter where you are, or what you're doing, "Every knee shall bow and every tongue confess Him," (Philippians 2:16). "For the Lord Himself shall descend from heaven with a shout, with the voice of the arch angel, and with the trump of God; and the dead in Christ shall rise first: Then we which are alive and remain shall be caught up together with them in the clouds to meet the Lord in the air and so shall we ever be with the Lord," (1 Thessalonians 4:16).

Get your house in order, get your ticket signed. He's coming back with power and great glory and judgment against His enemies. Be ready when He comes again. He said, "Surely I come quickly. Amen. Even so come Lord Jesus," (Revelation 3:20).

## Why Am I a Christian?
## II Timothy 4:6-8 NKJV

**Text:** For I am now ready to be offered and the time of my departure is at hand. I have fought a good fight, I have finished my course, I have kept the faith: henceforth there is laid up for me a crown of righteousness, which the Lord, the righteous judge, shall give me at that day; and not to me only, but unto all them also that love his appearing.

**Introduction:** Let us take mental flight to a Roman prison in AD 66. There the great missionary Paul is captive under Nero Caesar. This is the eve of Paul's martyrdom. A fellow prisoner approaches Paul (one who has committed a real crime), 'I hear you are to be executed tomorrow because you claim to be a Christian but you can escape death if you deny this Jesus and declare loyalty to Caesar. Obviously, He (Jesus) cannot save you. Look at what happened to his 12 disciples. Andrew was crucified on an X shaped cross. Bartholomew was skinned alive. The elder James was beheaded by Herod and the younger James was sawed in pieces. Judas Iscariot hung himself. Jude was killed with arrows. Matthew was murdered in Ethiopia. Peter was crucified hanging upside down, Philip was hanged in Hierapolis. Simon too was crucified. Thomas was speared to death in India and John was banished to the Island of Patmos. Even your Lord Jesus was executed, killed by the shame and agony of crucifixion. Paul, why do you insist on following such a treacherous, deadly path?' Paul replied, 'Sir, you have told me why I should not be, now let me tell you why I am a Christian.'

**Title: Why I am a Christian**

**Definition:** Christian (*Christeeonous*) or one who imitates Christ is a person professing belief in Jesus as the Christ of God, the Alpha and Omega the Anointed One, the Messiah, Emanuel, the fulfillment of the prophets, the Son of the Living God the Savior of the world, Mary's baby, the Lilly of the Valley, the Bright and Morning Star, the Rose of Sharon and the Prince of Peace.

Where did it all begin? The church began at Matthew 16:16 when Peter said, "Thou art the Christ, the Son of the living God." The movement known as Christianity began at Acts 11:25 and 26. Luke writes, "Then departed Barnabas to Tarsus, for to seek Saul: And when he had found him, he brought him unto Antioch. And it came to pass that a whole year they assembled themselves with the church and taught much people. And the disciples were called Christians first in Antioch." Those who despised the followers of Jesus called them Christians to spite or insult them, but today we wear the name as a badge of honor.

I. Unlike other religions, Christianity is an individual enterprise. Christianity is the religion of those who accept Jesus Christ as God incarnate, are guided by the Holy Spirit, and participate in the fellowship of the Christian Church.

1. Judaism is hereditary or corporate. Judaism as a religion is a belief in one universal God as creator, conceived of as personal. It interprets history as God's covenanted choice of the Jews to be the vehicle of His revelation and ultimate rule. The basis of this revelation was made on Mount Sinai when the Ten Commandments were delivered to Moses in the context of the teaching of the Pentateuch.

2. Islam is nationalistic or federated. It is a religious and social system based on the teachings of Mohammed as preserved in the Koran and the Sunna. Mohammed was convinced of the falsity of traditional Arab idolatry.

3. Christianity involves personal ratification to God through Jesus Christ who gave Himself, a propitiation for our sins.

II. In other words, Christianity is not a biological or physiological expression. We are not born Christian instead we make our entry as sinners because of Adam's original sin.

1. I am not a Christian because my mother and father are Christians.

2. Nor because of genealogy passed through X and Y chromosomes in the blood lines of generations now gone.

3. I cannot expect to see the kingdom of Heaven on the merits of family members. In fact, we are encouraged to forsake all and follow Christ.

4. Someone will ask, "How does one become a Christian?"
   The Bible tells us, "Believe on the Lord Jesus Christ and
   thou shalt be saved and thy house," (Acts 16:31). This
   motivates me to believe that I and I alone have ultimate
   responsibility to live a godly life so as to enter the strait
   gate.

III. Christianity cannot be achieved through associations.

1. Membership in the church is important, but not the
   answer to your soul salvation.

2. Your name on the role of circles, societies, fraternities
   and sororities will not include your name in the lamb's
   book of life.

3. Many years of service to the church and community
   are admirable, but not adequate for admission into the
   kingdom.

4. To be a Christian, we suffer and struggle to hear the
   master say as He said to the woman who washed His
   feet with her tears and wiped them dry with her hair.
   Thy faith hath saved thee (Luke 7:50).

IV. Christianity is priceless

1. The rich young ruler could not part with his treasure and
   fortified his true inheritance, eternal life.

2. In the temple, the widow's mite of faith delighted the
   Savior who equated her gift superior to all others.

3. Peter and John lacked silver and gold but gave a lame man healing through and he went away leaping and jumping.

4. My Lord said, "What would it profit a man to gain the entire world and yet lose his soul. Or what can a man give in exchange for his soul," (Mark 8:36).

V. Sacraments and office do not make me a Christian.

1. Not by Baptism, Holy Communion or feet washing, am I a follower of Christ. Those are the fringe benefits.

2. Nor that I am an officer of the church or minister of the Gospel. I'm convinced everybody who claims they are going to heaven is not necessarily going. Position, election or status a Christian does not make.

VI. I am a Christian because I choose to be.

1. No one had to force me, no one could compel me, and it was a personal choice. God allows us free will to do that which we choose so that our allegiance would be voluntary.

2. We are sinners by nature. We embrace Christian by choice. We entered the world lost in darkness. Through the precious blood of Jesus, we are rescued by grace.

3. I tried other ways. The way of the world, the way of the streets, money, and friends. I chased possessions, glory, and fame to find happiness, but nothing worked.

4.  One day I was burdened; my mind was ill at ease; I was searching for an answer. I heard it in the trees and they whispered to me: God is the answer in the time of need.[38]

**Conclusion:** Paul, the disciples and other great men and women of faith did not die in vain. I believe this occasioned the apostle to tell the Corinthian church, "Therefore, my beloved brethren, be ye steadfast, unmovable, always abounding in the work of the Lord, forasmuch as ye know that your labor is not in vain in the Lord," (I Corinthians 15:58).

Paul was beheaded on Nero's chopping block the next day. He was a good and faithful servant unto death. He must have heard the Lord say to John the Beloved, "You shall have tribulation but be thou faithful unto death and I will give thee a crown of life," (Revelation 2:10).

The same question asked of Paul by the inmate almost 2000 years ago is being asked today by a lost generation. Why are you a Christian in 2019? Shall you say because my Mom was or because everybody else is? I shall say because God delivered me from the quick sands of iniquity and rose from the grave with all power in His hand. My testimony will be because Jesus broke day light in my dark soul. I will declare because His yoke is easy, and His burden is light. He is the rock that the builders refused.

---

[38] R. H. Goodrastfur, "God is the Answer," *Mountain of Fire and Miracles Ministries Gospel Hymn Book*, Books on Goggle Play, 697.

Now He is the Chief Cornerstone. I'm glad to report to a sin cursed world... Jesus is the reason why I am a Christian.

# What's Love Got to Do with It?
## 1 John 4:7-8 NKJV

**Text:** Beloved, let us love one another: For love is of God: and everyone that loveth is born of God, and knoweth God. He that loveth not knoweth not God; for God is love.

**Exposition:** In approximately 100 A.D., John the beloved disciple, wrote this epistle or open letter to the universal church. John was stationed in Ephesus after his exile on the isle of Patmos. John was the bishop and founder of many churches in that region and this first of three letters are pastoral in nature or sermonic in scope.

In 1 John, the most visible reoccurring theme is love. The evangelist intertwines this theme throughout his letter. He encourages us to love our brothers and sisters but not the world and the things in the world. He invites us to "Behold what manner of love the Father has given us, that even though we are sinners by nature, He has caused us to be called the sons (and daughters) of God," (2 Corinthians 6:18).

**Introduction:** In 1984, pop icon Anna Mae Bullock *aka* Tina Turner found reason to differ with St. John. For 20 years she had suffered through an abusive relationship with her drug induced power crazed husband, Ike Turner. She had given her all and received little in return but contempt, violence and neglect. Over the years, such mean treatment caused Tina to become numb, rebel and fight back. In 1979, she divorced Ike and started again from scratch with nothing but her name. Nearly five years later she released a single that seemed to sum up her feelings about those dark years of her life. The song became an international smash hit, topping the charts worldwide. The chorus asks, "What's love got to do with it?

What's love but a second-hand emotion? What's love got to do with it? Who needs a heart when a heart can be broken?"[39]

Who would have known that such lyrics would make people rush out to record stores and buy Tina's song? Was it the haunting beat that caught everyone's attention? Was it her sultry voice that was the new rave of the 80's or was it the theme of the song, the rhetorical question: What's love got to do with it? Listen to a few more lines, "I've been thinking about a new direction, but I'm glad to say I've been thinking about my own protection, it scares me to feel this way but "What's love got to do with it?"[40]

This song was the most poignant hit of the 1980s. In a seemingly loveless society, where evil prospers and hate advances, where the wicked gain and the righteous suffer, where every man is for himself, where an eye for an eye, a

---

[39] Terrence Britton, *What's Love Got to Do With It?*, (written for Tina Turner), Chicago Soul Cellar, 1985.
[40] Ibid.

tooth for a tooth philosophy rules, in this world bent on destruction the question remains …

## What's Love Got to Do with It?

**Definition:** Someone has declared that love is the most overused word in the English language. Love is also the most misinterpreted word in our vocabulary. Many people talk about love but don't really know, what it is. They generally equate love with the special way someone makes them feel. That's why there's such a thin line between love and hate.

Many times, young people say they are in love with someone this week and in love with someone else next week. Are they just too young to know anything about love? I often wonder does anyone really know what love is or isn't to someone else? Merriam-Webster declares that love is, "Strong affection, warm attraction based on desire, to feel passion, devotion or tenderness, to take pleasure in something or someone."[41] This is a superficial definition. Obviously, love is many feelings, many experiences, many emotions, many memories many different things to many people. But in our sick world today, what's love got to do with it?

---

[41] Merriam-Webster, https://www.merriam-webster.com/dictionary/love?src=search-dict-box.

I.   Has love played out? Is love passé? Just look at our world today, look at the violence and pain that permeates our society. Just consider all of man's sin and corruption. Think about the atrocities of man's inhumanity to his fellowman, and you too will wonder, what's love got to do with it?

1.   September 11, 2001, revealed to us that everyone is not in love with the United States of America. We retaliated by invading Afghanistan and leveling the country. We decided that we could best love our country by destroying someone else's country.

2.   In Iraq, Saddam Hussein held United Nations inspectors at bay with an invisible war chest of lethal weapons of mass destruction. President Bush employed the full arsenal of United States air, naval and ground fire power to drive Saddam Hussein out and purge the land of the threat of chemical warfare. In the Syrian Civil War, 80 percent of the citizens remaining in the war ravaged nation have no running water, electricity, communications and educational system.[42] Because of government tariffs on imports, many American farmers don't know if they can pay their mortgages. Trump

---

[42] Joshua Hammer, "Is a Lack of Water to Blame for the Conflict in Syria?," *Smithsonian Magazine*, https://www.smithsonianmag.com/innovation/is-a-lack-of-water-to-blame-for-the-conflict-in-syria-72513729/.

claims his intention is to "Make America great again," but the citizens wonder, what's love got to do with it?

3.   The news media and tabloids are boiling over with evidence of a world devoid of love. Headlines declare the breakups and setbacks of celebrities torn apart by vanity, selfish pride and adultery.   Movie stars get married and divorced almost overnight.   Courthouse statistics reveal that one in every four marriages will end in divorce after only five years.[43]

4.   Where is love when our nation reeks with bigotry, hate, and racism?   In Virginia white nationalist marched through the campus of the University of Virginia carrying torches chanting, "Jews will not replace us." In El Paso, Texas a hate driven racist killed 22 Mexican men, women, and children who he claimed were "invading America."[44]

------

[43] Avvo, Marriage and Divorce Statistics, https://www.avvo.com/legal-guides/ugc/marriage-divorce-statistics.

[44] Rosa Flores and Michelle Krupa, "The El Paso Shooting is Exactly What Descendants of a 1915 Massacre at the US-Mexico Border had Warned About," *CNN,* https://www.cnn.com/2019/08/08/us/texas-matanza-descendants-el-paso-shooting/index.html.

5.   In the United States, 129 teenagers commit suicide every day.[45]   A homicide will occur every 12.8 minutes.[46] Every 9 seconds a woman in the U.S. is assaulted or beaten.[47]   One out of every three Black boys born today can expect to go to jail during their lifetime.[48]

## What's Love Got to Do with It?

II. This list goes on.   We could site hundreds of examples of hate, violence and inhumanity occurring in our world today. Love is waning.   Love seems to be in trouble.   Love is being butchered and battered around the globe.   The musical genius Stevie Wonder once wrote, "Love's in need of love today."[49] And though love seems to be fading and obsolete, the truth is, we all need love?   We must have love!   We can't survive without love!

---

[45] Ibid.

[46] American Foundation for Suicide Prevention, "Suicide Claims More Lives Than War, Murder, and Natural Disasters Combined," https://afsp.donordrive.com/index.cfm?fuseaction=cms.page&id=1226&eventGroupID=9AA19459-C880-0E26-61312B15147B2E0A&cmsContentSetID=D5C4DC12-C299-258B-B0B6FCF9EF015CE0.

[47] New Hope, "Facts About Domestic Violence," http://www.new-hope.org/facts-about-domestic-violence/?gclid=CjwKCAjwtajrBRBVEiwA8w2Q8KqWWIw6QCgafvbY7rXU JdLVaTY2RliZ4lldBknRvBDsn5EhcNGR0RoCI70QAvD_BwE.

[48] American Civil Liberties Union, "Mass Incarceration," https://www.aclu.org/issues/smart-justice/mass-incarceration

[49] Stevie Wonder, *Love's in Need of Love Today*, Songs in the Key of Life, 1976.

1. Love is as important to the soul as water is to the body. Whereas the body is composed of two-thirds water, the soul is composed completely of love. Love is to the soul as sunlight is to the roses. It makes the spirit grow, stretch forth, and one day bloom. We must have love. It is essential for the soul's existence. As the car needs fuel to run, the soul needs *love* to motivate itself.

2. Nothing in this universe is complete without love. No victory is won without love. Love is a victory within itself, for we must overcome our natural instincts to sin and transgress before we can truly love. Teach a child the hidden truths of science, the great wisdom of world literature, the wonders of modern medicine and the prowess of athletics, yet neglect to show him compassion, respect and love, then you have failed the child. You have created nothing more than a well-trained, educated fool.

3. It was therefore an emergency when Tina asked the question, "What's love got to do with it?" This is in essence, a cry for help. This is a SOS for assistance. This is someone on the edge of destruction. Someone in need of a blessing, someone in need of a friend. This is a question asked by someone with a wounded heart and a troubled soul.

4. This is a groan from a divorcee in the dark lonely night. This is a widowed person's teardrop falling on a cold pillow. The AIDS victim, cast out by society asks,

"What's love got to do with it? How does love relate to my being ostracized by family and friends?

5.  The single mother abandoned by the boyfriend who told her not to worry; now she's alone raising a baby on her own. She wonders, "What's love got to do with it?"

6.  The senior citizen, who gave the best years of her life to her family. She cooked, cleaned, and raised her children unselfishly. Now she's in the way, confined to a rest home, forgotten by family and friends. She rocks in her chair and wonders, "What's love got to do with it?"

7.  That homeless man, wondering from pillar to post, being run out of buildings and neighborhoods, shackled by the chains of poverty and displacement. He makes his bed out of cardboard under a bridge and wonders, "What's love got to do with it?"

8.  The young man on the streets slinging drugs in the hood, throwing gang signs and living a life of crime. Momma can't tell him to stop, she parties all the time. Daddy's gone, ain't seen him since he was a baby boy. His brothers and sisters are depending on him to pay the rent to a slum landlord who lives on the rich side of town and refuses to fix the roof. Little brother always packs a hand gun in his coat. He wonders, "What's love got to do with it?"

III. Yes the clouds seem full and ready to burst forth with gale rains of sadness and sorrow, vengeance and hate. But behind every storm cloud the sun awaits his turn. Yes the flood gates of mankind's suffering and oppression seem ready to burst forth and overflow the banks of brotherhood. But, who can oppose God? For God is love, and if God is love, (He Himself) then Love is God, (who can never be defeated). Therefore love is greater than any force that might come against us. Love is the most powerful substance in the universe. In fact, in the beginning love created the heavens and the earth. Every thought, every word, every act of God is an expression of unconditional love.

1. What's love got to do with it? Paul said, "I am persuaded that neither death nor life; nor angels nor principalities, nor power, nor things present nor things to come, nor heights nor depths nor any creature shall be able to separate us from the love of God, which is in Christ Jesus our Lord," (Romans 8:33).

2. I asked Jude, "What's love got to do with it?" Jude said, "Keep yourselves in the love of God, looking for the mercy of our Lord Jesus Christ unto eternal life," (Jude 1:21).

3. I asked John, "What's love got to do with it?" John said, "If a man say's, I love God, and hate his brother, he is a liar: For he that loveth not his brother whom

he hath seem, how can he love God whom he hath not seen," (1 John 4:20)?

4. I asked Peter, "What's love got to do with it?" Peter said, "Seeing ye have purified your souls in obeying the truth through the spirit unto unfeigned love of the brethren, see that ye love one another with a pure heart fervently," (1 Peter 1:22).

5. I asked the Hebrew writer, "What's love got to do with it?" The writer said, "Let brotherly love continue; be not forgetful to entertain strangers: for thereby some have entertained angels unawares," (Hebrews 13:1-2).

**Conclusion:** I want the whole world to know who has the final word on love, true love. Not that stuff on TV, not *Eros*. Not that stuff at family reunions, not *Philos*. Not Facebook love, but the real thing, *Agape* love. That is permanent love, sacrificial love, pure and unconditional love.

Jesus Christ is the ambassador of love. He said, "Therefore doth My Father love Me, because I lay down my life that I might take it up again," (John 10:17). Jesus Christ said, "A new commandment I give unto you that ye love one another as I have loved you," (John 13:34). The lover of My soul said, "Greater love hath no man than this that a man lay down his life for his friends," (John 15:13).

I know what love has done for me. When I was down and

out, love lifted me. When I was not fit to live and not ready to die, love saved me. When I was sinking deep in sin, love rescued me. When I was sick and could not get well, love healed me. The Captain of the seas heard my despairing cry when I was lonely and love befriended me.

You want to know what's love got to do with it? "For God so loved this world that He gave His only begotten Son that whosoever believeth on Him should not perish but have everlasting life," (John 3:16). Love made Him heal the sick and raise the dead. Love opened blind eyes and unclogged deaf ears. Love caused a dead friend to rise from the tomb. Love made the Sea of Galilee peaceful and still in the midst of a storm. Love stood trial in my place. Love died on an old rugged cross all day long. Love not nails held Jesus to the cross for a wretch like me. Love died on Friday evening. But love rose from the dead on Sunday morning. Love still has all power in His Hands.

**Poet:** Frederick Whitfield declared, "There is a name I love to hear, I love to sing its worth. It sounds like music is my ear, the sweetest name on earth. Oh, how I love Jesus, Oh, how I love Jesus, Oh, how I love Jesus, because He first loved me."[50]

---

[50] Ibid, Whitfield.

## Something to Die For
## Revelation 6:9 NIV

**Text:** And when he had opened the fifth seal, I saw under the altar the souls of them that were slain for the word of God, and for the testimony, which they held.

**Title: Something to Die For**

**Exposition:** In the 1st Century AD the Christian church experienced rapid growth. Through the preaching of the gospel by the apostles and many other disciples of Christ, thousands upon thousands of souls were won for our Savior. The Christian movement was forging ahead and spreading like wild fire. Yet in the days of the early church, as in our present age, any new movement was sure to meet with misunderstanding, disbelief, scrutiny, rumors, accusation, controversy and persecution. It is from this venue that the author of the Revelation of Jesus Christ writes.

Our author, John the beloved disciple, had witnessed much persecution during his lifetime. He witnessed the Roman occupation of Judah. He witnessed the plot by Jewish leadership to kill Jesus, implemented by the Romans at Jerusalem. He even witnessed the Roman blockade of Jerusalem and its complete destruction in 70 AD. His fellow disciples had met with violence and martyrdom. Andrew, Peter and Simon were brutally crucified. Bartholomew (aka Didymus the twin) was skinned alive. The elder James was beheaded, and the younger James was sawed in pieces. Judas Iscariot hung himself. Jude was executed by a firing squad with arrows. Matthew was stabbed to death in Ethiopia. Phillip was hung in Hierapolis, Thomas was speared to death and Paul was beheaded in Rome.

But this John found special favor with God. His character in the gospels portrays him as an obedient follower rather than a leader. A passive, humble gentleman, who watched Jesus Christ intently and walked closely with him delivering to us the most telling portrait of Jesus Christ as the God man of Galilee. It is for this reason that John the beloved was exiled and banished to the Island of Patmos rather than executed by Domitian Caesar. Sixty years after the execution of Jesus Christ at Jerusalem, we find John forced into exile on a lonely deserted strip of land in the Aegean Sea. Ten miles long and six miles wide, Patmos was a prison colony 40 miles southwest of Miletus. It is on the sandy shores of Patmos that John is said to have written the words of eschatological apocalypse or warnings of the coming of the end of time as we know it.

**Introduction:** Over the last 20 centuries many have been baffled by the themes of Revelation. Is each word to be taken in its literal form or is there some secret code to John's writings? Were his letters delivered to the churches without being tampered with? Or, were they first being read or possibly censored by Roman officials?

Then there are questions about John that we must ask ourselves. Being confined to a deserted island for almost a decade, is it possible that John could have developed some mental disorder that caused him to write such, livid, vivid, incredible, unbelievable, controversial mayhem and chaos? Could the author have been a paranoid schizophrenic? Could the author have been bipolar or delusional? Did he experience illusions of grandeur? Could John have been a manic-depressive or even an obsessive-compulsive?

Then we must wonder to whom John was writing. Was his letter intended for those who had already suffered persecution in his day? Or, was John writing to generations yet unborn, those who would take up the blood-stained banner and follow Jesus Christ even unto the ends of the world?

**Transition:** However we view John, we must acknowledge that he was a brave man; a strong and courageous soldier of the cross. One who was willing to go all the way for Christ? John lived as if he had something to die for.

**Exegesis:** In our text today, the Revelator shares with us a visual perspective of the Lion of Judah opening the 5th seal. The previous four seals revealed conquest, war and bloodshed, famine and pestilence, wholesale death and destruction. In the 5th seal the mood of the text changes from that of confrontation to an impasse of comfort and blessed assurance. For in the midst of the great vision John witnessed the souls of those who had been slain for the gospel of salvation, the word of God and the testimony, which they held. He saw them stretched out under the great alter in heaven, at the feet of King Jesus. Yet, they did not perish in vain, for they all had something to die for.

1. In our lives as Christians it is incumbent upon every one of us that we be not ashamed to bear witness of Jesus Christ. For Paul writes to the church at Rome, "I am not ashamed of the Gospel of Jesus Christ for it is the power of God unto salvation," (Romans 1:16). To Timothy he writes, "Be thou not ashamed of the testimony of our Lord...but be thou partaker of the afflictions of the gospel according to the power of God," (2 Timothy 1:8).

    a. We must bear witness of Him before our families. We must bear Him witness before our friends. We must start in our homes. Someone has said, 'Charity begins at home and spreads abroad.' We can't do much for that man in the streets while that man in our house is lost in his sins. The gospel message must be preached at home before it will be effective abroad.

    b. We must be His witness on our jobs. This does not mean that we must disrupt the work environment and evangelize to a coworker. What it does mean is we should carry ourselves as saints, as Christians and as children of God. We should treat our co-workers with such respect, esteem, and humanity that they cannot help but ask, "Are you a Christian?"

c. Bear him witness with your friends. Let them see the change in your life. Let them see how happy you are in Christ. If they ask you how you are doing, tell them that you are blessed. Don't be ashamed to let them see your new walk and hear your new talk. When they ask you to do things that you used to do, don't be afraid to tell them that you are a new creature in Christ, "Old things are passed away, look, He makes all things new," (2 Corinthians 5:17).

d. Bear him witness at church. Let people know that you did not come to see who is present. Let them know that you did not come to look good. Let them know that you're not here for form or fashion but that you have come to give thanks and praise to the Most High God. Tell somebody that God has been good to you, and that you've been washed in the blood of the lamb.

e. In every walk of life, in the streets, at school, at play, in whatever situation life casts upon you, remember, Jesus Christ said, "Ye are the light of the world. A city that is set on a hill cannot be hid. Let your light so shine before men, that they may see your good works and glorify your Father which is in heaven," (Matthew 5:14,16).

2. And though you do your best and give your all and all for Jesus Christ, sometimes in our lives we too (like John and the

saints of old) will be laughed at, unappreciated, ridiculed, and persecuted, some even killed for Christ's sake

a.  Families will turn and walk away. Doors will close when you walk into the house. Relatives will avoid you. Brother and sister will stop calling you. Mates will ask what's wrong with you. BFF's might goes so far to say "You're not fun like you used to be."

b.  People at work will test you to see if you are committed. They will say and do things to you to try and upset you, to see if you will revert to your former self.

c.  Friends will shun you on one hand and try to tempt you on the other hand. Fake friends will try to get you to take one more nostalgic stroll back down memory lane.

d.  Church folks will talk about you, laugh at you, search your record and remember when you used to be in the streets, remember when you used to be in sin. The folks, who ought to be helping you up, will put your faith to the hard test.

e.  Enemies will call you a holy roller, a goody-goody, a Jesus Christ freak, everything but a child of God. They will try to assassinate your personal character. Imps will encamp all about you, on every leaning side. Employing the words of their sharp-edged tongues, they will attempt to murder your good name for Jesus Christ's sake.

f.  "As it is written, for thy sake we are killed all the day long; we are accounted as sheep for the slaughter,"

(Romans 8:36). In spite of this be encouraged, for King David declared, "The Lord is my light and my salvation; whom shall I fear? The Lord is the strength of my life of whom shall I be afraid? When the wicked even mine enemies and my foes gather against me to eat up my flesh, they stumbled and fell," (Psalm 27:1-2). Paul encouraged us saying, "Therefore I beseech you to be ye steadfast, unmovable, always abounding in the work of the Lord, forasmuch as ye know that your labor is not in vain in the Lord," (1 Corinthians 15:58).

**Transition:** These patriarchs convince me, we have something to die for.

3.  Martin Luther King, Jr once said, "If a man has not discovered something that he will die for, he is not fit to live"[51] Socrates said, "The unexamined life is not worth living."[52] Argentine Civil Rights champion Ernesto Che Guevara said, "We cannot be sure of having something to live for unless we are willing to die for it."[53]

---

[51] Martin Luther King, Jr., "Address at the Freedom Rally at Cobo Hall," Birmingham, 1963, (Detroit: Stanford University, 1963).

[52] Socrates, "Socrates and Happiness: Explanations on the Good Life," https://www.the-philosophy.com/unexamined-life-worth-living-socrates.

[53] Ernesto Che Guevara, "Che Guevara Quotes," *BrainyQuote.com*, BrainyMedia Inc, 2019.
https://www.brainyquote.com/quotes/che_guevara_746563.

a. All these great minds throughout time in memorial have said and are saying to us today, there is a real purpose for our life. There is a reason for our living. We all have an assignment given to us from the foundations of the world. Stay on the bloody battlefield of life. Continue to wage the good fight of faith. There is a higher purpose. "Therefore, press toward the mark for the prize of the high calling of God in Christ Jesus," (Philippians 3:14).

b. Though we suffer down here in this barren land of despair and grief, "Be thou faithful unto death, and ye shall receive a crown of life," (Revelation 2:10).

- Wait on the Lord through tribulations.
- Though the evil ones seem to advance, wait on Him
- Though you suffer great trials dark on every hand
- Though many innocent souls lay prostrate under the altar of heaven
- Though they scandalize your name. Wait on Him.
- Though they lie on you
- Though they laugh at you
- Though they attack you from every angle. Wait on Him.
- Though they smile in your face and stab you in your back.
- Though they build you up just to see you fall.

- Though they turn your friends against you. Wait on Him.

- Though they say you're not going to make it, never forget, unearned suffering is redemptive. You shall reap what you sow (Galatians 6:7).

**Transition:** For under the altar of heaven here the souls of the blessed dead who die in Jesus Christ rest from their labors, the wicked shall cease from troubling and the weary shall be at rest. John the apostle of love declared, "For blessed are the dead that die in Christ from henceforth ...for they may rest from their labors and their works do follow them," (Revelation 14:13).

**Conclusion:** My beloved, under the altar of God, over in Shekinah Glory, with my mind's eye; I can see John over there, looking at the souls of the dead in Christ. Look there I see...Abraham, Isaac, and Jacob... Sarah, Rebecca, and Rachael... Moses, Joshua, and Ruth...Samuel, Ezra, and Nehemiah...Esther, Job, and David...Solomon, Isaiah, and Jeremiah...Ezekiel, Daniel, and Hosea...Joel, Amos, and Obadiah...Jonah, Micah, and Nahum...Habakkuk, Zephaniah, Haggai, Zechariah, and Malachi.

Look under the altar there is John the Baptist, Mother Mary, Zacchaeus, the woman with the issue of blood and blind Bartimaeus. I can see the three Hebrew boys and the twelve disciples. I see Martha, Lazarus, Deacon Stephen and look,

Paul, Silas, Elijah and Elisha are having a prayer meeting under the altar.

Don't you want to go and be with that heavenly host in glory? I'm going to be with the saints of old in the great by and by because, I've got something to die for. I've got someone to lay down my life for. His name is Wonderful, Counselor, Mighty God, Everlasting Father, and the Prince of Peace. Jesus Christ, the Son of Living God, who laid down His life for me has guaranteed that my labor will not be in vain. God has promised that I will be a crown of splendor and a royal diadem in His mighty hand.

# Glossary of Relevant Terms

1. *Christology* – study of Christ; the birth, life, ministry, mission, purpose of Christ's life while on Earth; The study of Christ's birth, death, burial and resurrection.

2. *Church* - is an association of people who share a particular belief system. The term *church* originated from the pre-Christian Germanic *kirika*. The term later began to replace the Greek *ekklesia*.

3. *Communion* - the rite that Christians perform in fulfillment of Jesus' instruction to do in memory of him what he did at his Last Supper; Remembrance of the bread represented was for Christ's body that was bruised for man's transgressions and the wine drank represented Christ's blood shed for the sins of man.

4. *Conclusion* - is a final proposition, which is arrived at after the consideration of evidence, arguments or premises. The conclusion normally solidifies and summarizes the complete thought of what was presented in the sermon, idea, paper, etc.

5. *Didactic* – (Greek) to teach, moral instruction by means of sermon or homily.

6. *Discernment* - To have the Holy Spirit internal guidance to give you the ability of an inner knowing of good or evil or the answers to unknown.

7. *Doctrine* - A belief or tenet, especially about philosophical or theological matters concerning the church; the body of teachings of a religion, or a religious leader, organization, group or text. To discuss what it is that particular church or ministry believe and why.

8. *Exegesis* – explanation; to draw the meaning out of a given text; to extract or to examine.

9. *Exposition* - a genre in which the purpose is to inform, explain, describe or define; provides background information; To give the history of a passage of scripture; and most time is the first section in a sermon.

10. *Glossolalia* - or *speaking in tongues* is a phenomenon in which people speak in languages unknown to them.

11. *Hermeneutics* - the science of interpretation and understanding of texts.

12. *Introduction* - an opening section of a piece of literature or a way to introduce a thought, story or sermon.

13. *Kerygma* – (*Greek*) Apostolic preaching the birth, life, death, and resurrection of Christ.

14. *Moshiach* – (*Hebrew*) The Anointed One; Messiah.

15. *Ministry* - type of activity conducted by members of various faiths; the mission, the purpose the call of work, service, activity that is performed by those individuals God has chosen for such work; The process of evangelism, building up, serving others, and doing the will of God on behalf of the Kingdom of God.

16. *Oracle* - An oracle is a person or persons considered to be the source of wise counsel or prophetic opinion; an infallible authority, usually spiritual in nature and speaks on behalf of God.

17. *Pericope* – a small passage of scripture that is used in textural reference that completes a thought.

18. *Pneuma* – (*Greek*) Breath, Holy Spirit.

19. *Preaching* – the deliverance of sermons are usually, but not always, delivered in a house of worship, most of which have a pulpit or ambo, an elevated architectural feature. A sermon is also known as a homily. To give a scriptural text that can exhort, rebuke, encourage, motivates the listener to be inspired; to speak of the 'good news' of Jesus the Christ.

20. *Prophecy* - is the prediction of future events or the speaking of divine words (divine Revelation) through chosen human messengers (prophets).

21. *Ruach HaKodesh* – (*Hebrew*) Breath of God, God the Holy Spirit.

22. *Sermon* - is an oration by a prophet or member of the clergy. Sermons address a Biblical, theological, or religious topic, usually expounding on a type of belief or law.

23. *Servant* - is one who works, and often also lives, within the employer's household. Servant in ministry is one who helps, aids, minister to others by way of service; Servant is one willing to aid others on behalf of their master.

24. *Syllogism* - A syllogism is a kind of logical argument that applies deductive reasoning to arrive at a conclusion based on two or more propositions that are asserted or assumed to be true.

25. *Textual Preaching* - Textual preaching is taking a section of a scripture or chapter and will normally have a main theme or thought flowing through it. Will dissect a particular text revealing what is underneath, meaning of text, and uncover what the author's intent of the message was.

26. *Theodicy* - is a specific branch of theology and philosophy that attempts to reconcile the existence of evil or suffering in the world with the assumption of a benevolent God —i.e. the problem of evil. An attempt to reconcile the co-existence of evil and God may thus be called "a theodicy".

27. *Theology* – study of God; intellectual study of the person, character, mission and impact of God.

28. *Topical preaching* – is focusing on a topic and connecting several scriptures or a main topic idea together to emphasize the topic or focus of sermon.

29. *Transition* – a movement from one point to another that will help the listener to grasp the sermon and walk through it with the messenger.

30. *Worship* - usually refers to specific acts of religious praise, honour, or devotion, typically directed to a supernatural being such as a god or goddess. The reference a Christian observes in acknowledging and reverencing God by having a personal relationship with Him.

* Note all glossary terms retrieved from Merriam-Webster Dictionary Online; http://www.merriam-webster.com/dictionary/

# Bibliography

007. "Inside the World of James Bond."
     https://www.007.com/.

American Civil Liberties Union. "Mass Incarceration."
     https://www.aclu.org/issues/smart-justice/mass-
     incarceration.

American Foundation for Suicide Prevention. "Suicide Claims
     More Lives Than War, Murder, and Natural Disasters
     Combined."
     https://afsp.donordrive.com/index.cfm?fuseaction=cms.p
     age&id=1226&eventGroupID=9AA19459-C880-0E26-
     61312B15147B2E0A&cmsContentSetID=D5C4DC12-
     C299-258B-B0B6FCF9EF015CE0.

Avvo. "Marriage and Divorce Statistics."
     https://www.avvo.com/legal-guides/ugc/marriage-
     divorce-statistics.

Britton, Terrence. *What's Love Got to Do With It?* (written for
     Tina Turner). Chicago Soul Cellar, 1985.

Che Guevara, Ernesto. "Che Guevara Quotes."
     *BrainyQuote.com.* Brainy Media Inc, 2019.
     https://www.brainyquote.com/quotes/che_guevara_7465
     63.

Clifford, John. "The Anvil of God's Word."
     https://www.wholesomewords.org/poetry/biblepoems/an
     vil.html.

Dallek, Matthew Dallek. "LBJ Announced He Wouldn't Run Again: Political Chaos Ensued." https://www.history.com/news/lbj-exit-1968-presidential-race.

Deloitte. "Global Mobile Consumer Survey: US Edition 2018." https://www2.deloitte.com/us/en/pages/technology-media-and-telecommunications/articles/global-mobile-consumer-survey-us-edition.html.

Donne, John. "John Donne Quotes." *Brainy Quote.* https://www.brainyquote.com/quotes/john_donne_136861.

Dr. Huey P. Newton Foundation. *The Black Panther Party: Service to the People Programs,* ed. David Hilliard. Albuquerque: University of New Mexico Press, 2008.

Ebert, Roger. "Deep Cover." https://www.rogerebert.com/reviews/deep-cover-1992.

Ebert, Roger. "I Spy." https://www.rogerebert.com/reviews/i-spy-2002.

Goodrastfur, R. H. "God is the Answer." *Mountain of Fire and Miracles Ministries Gospel Hymn Book.* Books on Goggle Play, 697.

Hamblen, Stuart. "Sang by Mahalia Jackson, It Is No Secret What God Can Do." Universal Music Publishing Group, Hamblen Music Company.

Hammer, Joshua Hammer. "Is a Lack of Water to Blame for the Conflict in Syria?" *Smithsonian Magazine.* https://www.smithsonianmag.com/innovation/is-a-lack-of-water-to-blame-for-the-conflict-in-syria-72513729/.

174

Jackson, George B. *Ordination Training for Bi-vocational Clergy.* Thomasville: Pureheart Publishing Inc., 2017.

Jones, Tommy. "Look Where He Brought Me From." http://www.allgospellyrics.com/?sec=listing&lyricid=6717.

King, Jr., Martin Luther. "Champions of Human Rights: Martin Luther King Jr. (1929-1968)." *Voices for Human Rights.* https://www.humanrights.com/voices-for-human-rights/martin-luther-king-jr.html.

King, Jr., Martin Luther. "A Christmas Sermon on Peace." Beacon Broadside Press, December 24, 1967.

King, Jr., Martin Luther. "I've Been to The Mountaintop." Stanford: The Martin Luther King, Jr. Research and Education Research, 1968.

King, Jr., Martin Luther. "Martin Luther King, Jr. Quotes." *Brainy Quote.* https://www.brainyquote.com/quotes/martin_luther_king_jr_102371.

King, Jr., Martin Luther. "Quotes." https://www.goodreads.com/quotes/56448-if-we-do-an-eye-for-an-eye-and-a.

King, Jr., Martin Luther. "Quotes Martin Luther King, Jr." *AZ Quotes.* https://www.azquotes.com/quote/757999.

King, Jr., Martin Luther. "The Drum Major Instinct." Sermon, Ebenezer Baptist Church, Atlanta, 1968.

King, Jr., Martin Luther. "Triple Evils." *The King Philosophy.* https://thekingcenter.org/king-philosophy/.

King, Jr., Martin Luther. "When Peace Becomes Obnoxious." Sermon, Dexter Avenue Baptist Church, March 18, 1956.

LaNier, Carlotta Walls. *A Mighty Long Way*. New York: Ballantine Books, 1957.

Lowell, James Russell. "The Present Crisis." https://poets.org/poem/present-crisis.

Moore, Malcolm. "China: A Force Fit For a Superpower." *The Telegraph*. https://www.telegraph.co.uk/news/worldnews/asia/china/8251307/China-a-force-fit-for-a-superpower.html.

Newton, Isaac. "Newton's Law of Universal Gravitation." *Lumen Learning*. https://courses.lumenlearning.com/boundless-physics/chapter/newtons-law-of-universal-gravitation/.

Never Alone. "119 Hymnals." https://hymnary.org/text/ive_seen_the_lightning_flashing

Pickett, Ludie Carrington Day. "I've Seen the Lightening Flashes." https://www.hymnal.net/en/hymn/h/688.

Merriam-Webster. https://www.merriam-webster.com/dictionary/love?src=search-dict-box.

New Hope. "Facts About Domestic Violence." http://www.new-hope.org/facts-about-domestic-violence/?gclid=CjwKCAjwtajrBRBVEiwA8w2Q8KqWWIw6QCgafvbY7rXUJdLVaTY2RliZ4lldBknRvBDsn5EhcNGR0RoCI70QAvD_BwE.

Seeger, Pete. "All My Trials." *American Favorite Ballads*, Vol. 4, 1961.

Socrates. "Socrates and Happiness: Explanations on the Good Life." https://www.the-philosophy.com/unexamined-life-worth-living-socrates.

Traditional Negro Spiritual. "Ride on King Jesus." http://dailyprayer.us/Christian_song_lyrics/Christian_song_lyrics.php?s=ride_on_king_jesus.

Watts, Isaac. "Am I a Solider of the Cross." https://www.hymnal.net/en/hymn/h/468.

Whitfield, Frederick. "Oh How I Love Jesus." *Public Domain*, 1855. https://library.timelesstruths.org/music/Oh_How_I_Love_Jesus/.

Wonder, Stevie. *Love's in Need of Love Today*. Songs in the Key of Life, 1976.

Yancey, Philip D. *The Bible Jesus Read.* Grand Rapids: Zondervan, 1999.

George Bernard Jackson is the fifth of six children born to Dr. William T. and Pearlena M. Jackson of Salisbury, NC. He is a 1980 graduate of Chester Senior High School in Chester, SC. He graduated from North Carolina Central University in Durham, NC with a Bachelor of Arts in Political Science.

Jackson received the Master of Divinity degree with honors in May 1996 from Shaw Divinity, Raleigh, NC. He later received the Doctor of Ministry degree from Friends International Christian University, Merced, CA in October 1998. In May 2009, Jackson received the Doctor of Ministry in Pastoral Care, Gardner-Webb University, Boiling Springs, NC.

In August 2001, Jackson founded Citadel of Faith Christian Fellowship, Thomasville, NC. He has been in ministry for 33 years and the pastoral ministry for 32 years. In November 2005, he founded United Cornerstone University and serves as president. A community activist, Jackson founded Martin Luther King Social Action Committee in 1993. In June 2013 he was elected Presiding Prelate of Citadel Ministries International Inc. overseeing 14 churches, in the U.S., and churches in Andhra Pradesh, India and Kenya, East Africa. Jackson was conferred a member the Order of the Long Leaf Pine Society, from Governor of North Carolina, December 2016.

He has dedicated this labor of love to the edifying of God's people and building the cherished "Beloved Community." Jackson is married to the lovely Superintendent Dr. Pamela Stanfield Jackson. They are building a legacy for six children and six grandchildren.

Other Books by Dr. George B. Jackson


*Tears of a Clown, 2013*

*I'll Meet You in Gethsemane, 2015*

*Ordination Training for Bi-vocational Clergy, 2017*